LOUIS MACNEICE

A critical study

Edna Longley

First published in 1988
by Faber and Faber Limited
3 Queen Square London WC1N 3AU
Reprinted with corrections 1996

Photoset by Wilmaset Birkenhead
Printed in England by Clays Ltd, St Ives plc

A CIP record for this book is available from the British Library

ISBN 0-571-13748-2

2 4 6 8 10 9 7 5 3 1

books by Louis MacNeice

COLLECTED POEMS
Edited by E. R. Dodds

SELECTED POEMS
Edited by Michael Longley

THE STRINGS ARE FALSE
An Unfinished Autobiography

LETTERS FROM ICELAND
With W. H. Auden

of related interest

LOUIS MACNEICE
A biography
by Jon Stallworthy

Contents

Acknowledgements

I am grateful to the Estate of Louis MacNeice, Faber and Faber Ltd, and Oxford University Press for permission to quote from the works of Louis MacNeice; and to the Estate of Louis MacNeice and the Bodleian Library for permission to quote from the unpublished letters of Louis MacNeice to E. R. Dodds.

Acknowledgements are also due to the following for permission to quote from copyright material:

W. H. Auden: extracts from 'The Orators' and 'Letter to Lord Byron' in *The English Auden: Poems, Essays and Dramatic Writings 1927–1939* (edited by Edward Mendelson) by permission of Faber and Faber Ltd and Random House Inc.
Hubert Butler: extract from *Escape from the Anthill* by permission of the author and Lilliput Press.
Geoffrey Grigson: extract from Introduction to *Poetry of the Present* by permission of Jane Grigson and Chatto and Windus.
Samuel Hynes: extracts from *The Auden Generation* by permission of the author and the Bodley Head.
Richard Johnstone: extract from *The Will to Believe* by permission of the author and Oxford University Press.
W. R. Rodgers: extract from 'Epilogue' to *The Character of Ireland* by permission of the Estate of W. R. Rodgers and Oxford University Press.
Stephen Spender: extract from *The Thirties and After* by permission of the author and William Collins Sons & Co.

Preface

Louis MacNeice (1907–63) is a central poet of the twentieth century. On the one hand, his poetry has absorbed the communal experiences of four decades; on the other, it fully enters our perennial life of the senses and the psyche. MacNeice believed in the poet as a maker, and in the humane significance of making 'good patterns'. Since he also thought the poet should be a blend of 'critic and entertainer', his patterns involve what he called 'twopence coloured': all that can be done with language as well as said in it. Perhaps the best way to sum up the advent and impact of MacNeice's poetry is to quote the opening of his well-known poem 'Snow': 'The room was suddenly rich . . .' In 1949 Geoffrey Grigson, formerly editor of the great thirties magazine *New Verse*, developed his own metaphor for a talent he had spotted from the start:

> there in these juvenilia [*Blind Fireworks*, 1929] were stretched to tautness criss-crossing wires of form with this spangled acrobat performing on them; and the cleverness, as one knows by this time, grew and strengthened itself into a capable and convincing rhetoric, beholden to much, yet chiefly to MacNeice himself. The wires were still silvery and still glittered. The icicles, the ice-cream, the pink and white, the lace and the froth and the fireworks were still there, but underneath the game was the drop, the space, and the knowledge.
>
> (Introduction to *Poetry of the Present*)

But not every critic is as alert as Grigson, and for various reasons MacNeice's reputation has developed unevenly. Chief among these is the tendency to brand one of his literary contexts with the name of another poet. The very titles of the following books marginalize MacNeice: Francis Scarfe's *Auden and After* (1942), Samuel Hynes's *The Auden Generation* (1976), the Macmillan Casebook *Thirties Poets: 'The Auden Group'* (1984). MacNeice never resented W. H. Auden's shadow. On the contrary, in *Modern Poetry* (1938) and earlier essays he evangelized on behalf of Auden and the new poetry in general. At the same time, neither these critical writings nor his own poetry can be produced in evidence of an aesthetic uniformly dictated by Auden. Nor, during at least half the decade, was MacNeice grouped with 'the inevitable trio' of poets – who were Auden, Stephen Spender and Cecil Day Lewis. Indeed Day Lewis's 'Postscript 1936' to *A Hope for Poetry* greeted MacNeice's *Poems* (1935) as representing something fresh: 'a return to the ideals of poetic integrity and artistic individualism'. And Francis Hope in 1964 saw his reputation as rising in inverse ratio to that of politicized poetry: 'the higher this uncommitted urban lyricist, modern but not contemporary, the further we are from the Left Book Club and the International Brigade' (Ian Hamilton (ed.), *The Modern Poet: Essays from 'The Review'*).

Hope overstates MacNeice's distance from collective thirties concerns. A MacNeice-centred view of the decade complicates rather than wholly contradicts the usual picture. This book will argue that, longer than other 'thirties poets', during the war years and into the early 1960s, MacNeice pursued the questions of 'commitment' and of poetry's obligation to the 'contemporary'. But if Spender and Day Lewis have gradually ceased to stand in MacNeice's light (which corrects the initial over-estimation of these poets as much as it reflects a change in literary attitudes), English critics have continued to tax him with being 'uncommitted' in a non-political sense. They suspect his acrobatics, moralize over his poetry's brilliant 'surface' and lack of a philosophical 'core'. This is the line broadly taken, for instance, by G. S. Fraser's 'Evasive Honesty: The Poetry of Louis MacNeice' (in *Vision and Rhetoric*, 1959), Ian Hamilton's (1963) essay in *A Poetry Chronicle*, and Stephen Wall's 'Louis MacNeice and the line of Least Resistance' (*The Review* 11–12, 1964). Such analysis often reads conflicts explored by the poetry as literal problems of the poet himself. 'Snow', for instance, does not so much surrender to surfaces as hold the 'drunkenness of things being various' in an infinitely delicate balance: 'There is more than glass between the snow and the huge roses.' Several philosophies are swallowed by the way in which 'between' both separates and joins. Similarly, the *plot* of *Autumn Journal* turns on a tension between evasion and commitment. William T. McKinnon in *Apollo's Blended Dream* (1971) and Terence Brown in *Louis MacNeice: Sceptical Vision* (1975) make amends to the metaphysical seriousness of

MacNeice's poetry. Brown simultaneously defends it against a related charge – compromise rather than evasion. He argues that 'the central determining factor in MacNeice's poetry and thought, far from being a decent, liberal, but rather commonplace agnosticism, was a tense awareness of fundamental questions, rooted in philosophical scepticism'. Since MacNeice himself distrusted the *a priori*, it is a productive approach to see the positions of his poetry, whether liberal or darkly doubtful, as won through imaginative struggle – at a time of great struggles.

But philosophical coherence is not the only coherence available to poetry. This book stresses MacNeice's own point that, as well as being essentially dialectical, his poetry is essentially dramatic. His important essay, 'Experiences with Images' (1949), contains a key statement:

> The word 'lyric' has always been a terrible red herring. It is taken to connote not only comparative brevity but a sort of emotional parthenogenesis which results in a one-track attitude labelled 'spontaneous' but verging on the imbecile. In fact all lyric poems, though in varying degrees, are *dramatic* – and that is two ways. (1) The voice and mood, though they may pretend to be spontaneous, are yet in even the most 'personal' of poets such as Catullus and Burns a *chosen* voice and mood, set defiantly in opposition to what they must still co-exist with; there may be only one actor on the stage but the Opposition are on their toes in the wings – and crowding the auditorium; your lyric in fact is a monodrama. (2) Even in what is said (apart from the important things unsaid) all poems, though again in varying degrees, contain an internal conflict, cross-talk, backwash, come-back or pay-off. This is often conveyed by sleight-of-hand – the slightest change of tone, a heightening or lowering of diction, a rhythmical shift or a jump of ideas. Hence all poems, as well as and because of being dramatic, are *ironic* (in the old Greek sense of 'dramatic irony'); poet and reader both know, consciously or unconsciously, the *rest* of the truth which lurks between the lines. And finally the lyric, which is thus dramatic and ironic, is also – it should go without saying – from the first and, above all, *symbolic*.

The English suspicion of MacNeice often derives from a puritanical objection to dramatic stylization, to the poet 'hiding' behind a façade. Thus Stephen Spender in 1967:

> The brilliant opaque surface which he exhibited in his behaviour remains . . . a problem for the reader in his work. It is not only that one tries vainly much of the time to penetrate the centre of MacNeice's own sensibility; one also finds oneself trying vainly to get at the centre of people and experiences he describes.

MacNeice's personal reserve was the product of profound reservations about the world around him. His poetic reserve is a function of dramatic technique.

Admittedly, MacNeice blurred the outline of his lyric theatre because, like Auden, he wrote too much. The 'volubility and generosity' which Grigson considers vital to the thirties generation can become a pseudo-fertility, as if it were the poet's duty simply to go on writing. Critics rightly condemn MacNeice's wordy dullness in some longer poems of the 1940s, *Ten Burnt Offerings* (1952) and *Autumn Sequel* (1954). However, one sign of a major poet is that he continually broods on the same obsessions and images, but finds different forms for them. MacNeice's true energy returned in *Visitations* (1957), more powerfully in *Solstices* (1961) and *The Burning Perch* (1963). In the two latter collections he finally purged an obsolete discursiveness, using techniques of 'parable' to dramatize the consciousness of 'Everyman' with new concentration.

MacNeice's stress on drama relates him to W. B. Yeats: a relationship written all over his pioneering study *The Poetry of W. B. Yeats* (1941), and one which will be highlighted in what follows. His relish of style is partly an Anglo-Irish relish. In *Modern Poetry* he declares an Irish prejudice when he prefers a 'controlled flamboyance of diction' to the Wordsworthian 'crusade for homespun'. Like Yeats's poetry, MacNeice's descends from the non-Wordsworthian branch of Romanticism. (Spender seems to be applying inappropriate criteria of 'sincerity'.) Philip Larkin, no mean stylist himself, thought of MacNeice as 'poetically a sophisticated, almost dressing-gowned figure, dropping epithets into place effortlessly and exactly'. MacNeice's Irishness, fundamental to his poetry, has often been invisible to English and American critics, or regarded merely as a decorative Celtic fringe. Thus Samuel Hynes refers to 'the tone of the professional lachrymose Irishman'. MacNeice's connection with the tears of Erin cannot be so simply formulated. Grigson shows greater understanding when he describes MacNeice as 'cut off in some degree and in some ways to his advantage by his Irishness and an Irish childhood, in spite of an English education'. On the other hand, with the erosion of the Anglo-Irish Protestant community in the South of Ireland, MacNeice's poetry has often been seen there as dealing with matters alien to Ireland – the Second World War for instance – and as Anglicized in manner. His work had a shaky history in anthologies of Irish poetry until the publication in 1986 of Paul Muldoon's *Faber Book of Contemporary Irish Poetry*, where he shares pride of place with Patrick Kavanagh.

Any danger of MacNeice's poetry sinking somewhere in the Irish Sea (a characteristic Anglo-Irish fate) has been averted by the fact that a new generation of poets has appeared from what the blurb of *Poems* (1935) called 'his Northern Ireland'. Since 1960 MacNeice's influence on Derek Mahon, Paul Muldoon and others has retrospectively helped to define his native context. In 1972 Mahon observed that his reputation has particularly 'come to rest' in the North, 'where his example has provided a frame of reference for a number of younger poets' (Introduction to *The Sphere Book of Modern Irish Poetry*). In the wake of the poets, critics from Ulster (Terence Brown, Peter McDonald) or informed about Ulster (William T. McKinnon) have begun to interpret MacNeice's cultural complexity (McKinnon's essay on MacNeice's father in *Honest Ulsterman* no. 73, 1983 is especially useful). MacNeice's own formulations run to paradox: 'I wish one could either *live* in Ireland or *feel oneself* in England', he wrote to E. R. Dodds in the 1940s. This conflict can be read negatively – the condition of being an outsider in two countries. Or, with Grigson, we can see it as artistically advantageous. Certainly, shifting attitudes to Ireland are integral to MacNeice's creative self-dramatization. Further, because MacNeice's poetry dramatizes polarities engendered by Ireland, such as that between belonging and alienation, it has become a focus on the literary wing of current debates about 'identity' in Northern Ireland.

MacNeice explains himself better than most poets, so the publication of his *Selected Literary Criticism* (1987) should underline his kinship with Yeats's 'identity in difference', and help to rescue him from some of the 'Procrustean' critical categories to which he objected. In *The Poetry of W. B. Yeats* a defence of the Crazy Jane poems modulates into a more personal testament:

> If a poet has been labelled serious, he must never be frivolous. If the poet has been labelled 'love poet', he is taken to be declining

> if he shows the Latin quality of 'salt'. If on the other hand a satirist starts writing from the heart, he is guilty of sentimentality. But the poet should not bother with this Procrustes who has to live by his bed. 'So I am to speak only as myself,' the poet might say, 'my whole self, and nothing but myself?' If you know what my whole self and my only self is, you know a lot more than I do. As far as I can make out, I not only have many different selves but I am often, as they say, not myself at all. Maybe it is just when I am not myself – when I am thrown out of gear by circumstances or emotion – that I feel like writing poetry.

To redirect 'Snow' again: MacNeice's poetry is 'more of it than we think, / Incorrigibly plural'. It reproduces the sensory assault of existence 'On the tongue on the eyes on the ears in the palms of one's hands'. He turns this inside out to imagine 'not-being'. On its socio-political level, his poetry distinguishes in a uniquely subtle way between what is owed to the individual and what to the community, thus living up to the promise of his statement in 1935: 'The individualist is an atom thinking about himself (Thank God I am not as other men); the communist, too often, is an atom having ecstasies of self-denial (Thank God I am one in a crowd).' On its metaphysical level, his poetry faces the whole issue of the self in the world:

> Windows between you and the world
> Keep out the cold, keep out the fright;
> Then why does your reflection seem
> So lonely in the moving night?
>
> ('Corner Seat')

And on its aesthetic level, his poetry reconciles traditionalism and Modernism. In a curious way MacNeice did more than other twentieth-century poets to test poetry against the century. He tested it against the claims of politics and philosophy, against the pressures of cities and war. And he did not take the outcome of these tests, or of anything else, for granted.

1
'Ireland, My Ireland'

I

MacNeice saw his origins in Ulster and Ireland as indelibly imprinting his life and work:

> But I cannot deny my past to which my self is wed,
> The woven figure cannot undo its thread.
>
> ('Valediction')

> Though yet her name keeps ringing like a bell
> In an under-water belfry.
>
> (*Autumn Journal* XVI)

'Carrick Revisited', a poem about returning to Carrickfergus where his father had been rector, enlists geology as a still stronger metaphor for irreversible design, for experiences laid down in the unconscious:

> Torn before birth from where my fathers dwelt,
> Schooled from the age of ten to a foreign voice,
> Yet neither western Ireland nor southern England
> Cancels this interlude; what chance misspelt
> May never now be righted by my choice.
>
> Whatever then my inherited or acquired
> Affinities, such remains my childhood's frame
> Like a belated rock in the red Antrim clay
> That cannot at this era change its pitch or name –
> And the pre-natal mountain is far away.

Yet all three quotations belong to dialectical structures, to the inner argument that makes MacNeice's Irishness, and his poetry, the product of pulls in contrary directions (which might be a description of Ulster itself). 'Carrick Revisited', like the earlier 'Carrickfergus' (1937), is less a literal memoir than a cultural and imaginative map. Thus 'western Ireland' represents family ties that became a mythic allegiance. Both MacNeice's parents had been brought up near Clifden in Connemara – 'the pre-natal mountain'. Louis and his sister Elizabeth liked to consider themselves western exiles in the North. As the 'first of [my] dream worlds' (*SAF*, p. 216) the West not only received its own poetic incarnations, but was the prototype for other Hy Brasils and Utopias in MacNeice's writing. 'Southern England' also enshrines myth. While at Sherborne preparatory school MacNeice 'read into this country of the Dorset–Somerset border a wealth of legend, mainly drawn from Malory' (*SAF*, p. 221). However, England principally represents fact: the facts of his educational, professional, and literary careers. In 1917 he went to Sherborne; in 1921 to Marlborough; and in 1926 to Merton College, Oxford. After Oxford he lectured in classics at Birmingham University (where E. R. Dodds was professor), then in Greek at Bedford College, London. From 1941 to 1961 he worked for the BBC, mainly as a producer and writer in the renowned Features Department. Up to his premature death in 1963 he contributed programmes on a part-time basis. He died of pneumonia as a result of going underground with sound-engineers who were recording effects for his last radio play, *Persons from Porlock*.

A different kind of poet might have left Ireland imaginatively as well as physically behind. It is significant that MacNeice often reflects on the relevance of a poet's or poem's 'background'. In *Modern Poetry* and elsewhere he attacks 'determinist critics' for equating the factors which *condition* poetry with its *cause*. Among his targets are: Marxists who explain poetry exclusively in terms of a merely 'general' social or economic context, and psychoanalytical critics who explain it exclusively in terms of 'a poet's psychological biography'. But beyond such exclusivities he took the Romantic view, given fresh licence by Freud, that poetry begins in childhood:

> The channels of my dreams determined largely
> By random chemistry of soil and air.
>
> ('Carrick Revisited')

As Dodds says in his preface to MacNeice's autobiography *The Strings are False* (written in the early 1940s but published posthumously): 'his continuing preoccupation with his own past . . . amounted almost to an obsession' (pp. 14–15). The poem 'Perdita', which includes another Ireland of the unconscious, personifies the compulsive lure of the lost:

> The glamour of the end attic, the smell of old
> Leather trunks – Perdita, where have you been
> Hiding all these years? Somewhere or other a green
> Flag is waving under an iron vault
> And a brass bell is the herald of green country
> And the wind is in the wires and the broom is gold.

Loss (his mother, his country, his first marriage) drew MacNeice to autobiography as a means of knitting fractures, though not solely for egocentric reasons: 'Maybe, if I look back, I shall find that my life is not just mine, that it mirrors the lives of the others – or shall I say the Life of the Other?' (*SAF*, p. 35). Under the impress of personal and public crises, MacNeice's autobiographies multiplied during the years 1937–41; his lyrical self-dramatization acquired more hinterland. Besides *Autumn Journal* and *The Strings are False* there are the short poems 'Carrickfergus' and 'Autobiography', the sequence 'Novelettes', and autobiographical passages in the prose compilations *I Crossed the Minch* (1938) and *Zoo* (1938). Even *Modern Poetry* incorporates 'My Case-Book': a history of his relationship with poetry from childhood up to residence in Birmingham; while *The Poetry of W. B. Yeats* obliquely defines aspects of its author's identity. Shortly before his death, as Dodds tells us, MacNeice was planning *Countries in the Air*, 'at once a new kind of autobiography and a new kind of travel book'. The surviving fragment, appended to *The Strings are False*, begins biblically: 'In the beginning was the Irish rain.'

2

MacNeice kept the past alive for artistic reasons, just as he cultivated dreams and nightmares. But the 'obsession' was itself conditioned by a childhood full of intense but often inexplicable feeling. 'Experiences with Images' – another instance of autobiographical criticism – dwells on the chain reaction between primary experience and its poetic afterglow:

> I was born in 1907 in Belfast and brought up on the northern shore of Belfast Lough, i.e., in a wet, rather sombre countryside where linen mills jostled with primitive rustic cottages and farmyard noises and hooters more or less balanced each other. Thus the factory entered my childhood's mythology long before I could place it in any social picture. As for the sea, it was something I hardly ever went on but there it was always, not visible from our house but registering its presence through foghorns. It was something alien, foreboding, dangerous, and only very rarely blue. But at the same time (since until I was ten I had only once crossed it) it was a symbol of escape. So was the railway which ran a hundred yards below our house but N.B. the noise of the trains – and this goes for the foghorns and the factory hooters also – had a significance apart from what caused that noise; impinging on me before I knew what they meant . . .
>
> These things sound trivial but they form an early stratum of experiences which persists in one's work just as it persists in one's dreams. Sea (i.e., the grey Lough fringed with scum and old cans), fields (i.e., the very small, very green hedged fields of Northern Ireland), factories (i.e., those small factories dotted through the agricultural patchwork), and gardens (i.e., my father's medium-sized lush garden with a cemetery beyond the hawthorn hedge), these things, being my earliest acquaintances, remain in *one* sense more real to me than, say, wide open spaces, downs, mountains, high cliffs or woods. For it is these former images which I am more likely to use 'instinctively'. (*SCLM*, pp. 158–9)

That passage does not simply catalogue a collection of random and rigid impressions. The Carrickfergus 'chemistry', or the chemistry between MacNeice and Carrickfergus, generated a true microcosm, rich in creative potential. Indeed, the 'cemetery beyond the hawthorn hedge' spans his entire poetry. Belfast Lough and the trains pointed towards his motif of the Quest, and towards the poems constructed as journeys or rides. The sea later gained further associations from a trip to Portstewart on the Antrim coast: 'suddenly around a corner or over a crest came a strong salt breeze and a rich smell of herring and there down below us was blueness, lumbering up against the wall of the fishermen's quay . . . exploding in white and in gulls' (*SAF*, p. 39). In 'Round the Corner' (1961) this experience is the starting-point for MacNeice's accumulated symbolism of the sea. That the Portstewart revelation took a long time to surface definitively in a poem, illustrates how this 'early stratum' remained in one sense geologically unstable, subject to changing imaginative pressures. This may reflect the multiple or gradual impact of the early images themselves. MacNeice's urban landscapes owe some of their sensuous and metaphorical density to 'the factory [entering] my childhood's mythology long before I could place it in any social picture'. He never resorts to the spray-on industrialism for which some poets of the 1930s deserved the tag 'pylon poets'. In fact his general social documentation was evidently fostered by this Northern Irish semi-industrial environment within which the natural and mechanical threw one another into vivid relief.

The relation between sound and the other dimensions of an image seems to have conditioned MacNeice's slow-release symbolism. 'Carrick Revisited', like 'Experiences with Images', suggests the poet's ear latent in the child receiving the transmissions of his world:

> Fog-horn, mill-horn, corncrake and church bell
> Half-heard through boarded time as a child in bed
> Glimpses a brangle of talk from the floor below
> But cannot catch the words.

More darkly, in 'The Ear' the proto-poet is a child powerless to block the unmediated noise of night. MacNeice's earliest poetry is a sound archive. The Juvenilia in the *Collected Poems*, i.e. what survives of *Blind Fireworks* (1929), include several poems which explore the 'purely physical meaning' of noises: train-noises, wind-noises, sea-noises, rook-noises, even (in 'Poussin', 'Evening Indoors' and 'Happy Families') the contrasting sounds of silence. 'River in Spate', originally entitled 'A Cataract conceived as the

March of Corpses', interprets the cold message of one water-noise:

The river falls and over the walls the coffins of cold funerals
Slide deep and sleep there in the close tomb of the pool,
And yellow waters lave the grave and pebbles pave its mortuary
And the river horses vault and plunge with their assault and battery . . .

This differs from a river in spate *symbolizing* a cataract of death. Here the sound controls the unfolding sense. 'Genesis', which reproduces sounds of creation, may hint at the aural genesis of MacNeice's own inspiration:

> A million whirling spinning-wheels of flowing gossamer,
> A million hammers jangling on the anvils of the sky,
> The crisp chip of chisels and the murmuring of saws
> And the flowing ripple of water from a million taps . . .

That workshop prefigures a poetry full both of onomatopoeic words and cadences, and of words for sounds: hooting, clang, jingles, 'dingle-dongle', twang, 'creaks and cawings', gulp, clatter, pop, click, boom, blare, crackle, cackle, clink, splash, bark, purr, roar, thrumming, yammering, 'tick by tick'. Later, MacNeice's radio plays and productions confirmed his consciousness of sound effects (as the circumstances of his death sadly indicate).

MacNeice's responsiveness *to* sound partly shaped his responsiveness *through* sound. *Blind Fireworks* experiments with assonance, rhyme, rhythm, refrain. 'The Creditor' (now the first poem in the *Collected Poems*) feels its way along through allied sounds and internal rhyme, the latter both feminine and consonantal in the following quotation:

> I lull myself
> In quiet in diet in riot in dreams,
> In dopes in drams in drums in dreams . . .

This reads like the verbal doodle of a poet 'lulled' or mesmerized by the music of words. Internal rhyme is a form of rhythmical punctuation or metrical emphasis which MacNeice virtually patented as a habitual device. 'River in Spate' points to its partly mimetic origin: the poem's impetus depends on sequences like 'lave–grave–pave', over which the surrounding assonance and alliteration pour. MacNeice developed the device to intensify a great variety of impressions. In 'Morning Sun' (1935) the visual receives the same treatment as the aural:

Everything is kissed and reticulated with sun
Scooped-up and cupped in the open fronts of shops
And bouncing on the traffic which never stops.

And the street fountain blown across the square
Rainbow-trellises the air and sunlight blazons
The red butcher's and scrolls of fish on marble slabs,
Whistled bars of music crossing silver sprays
And horns of cars, touché, touché, rapiers' retort, a moving cage,
A turning page of shine and sound, the day's maze.

The exaggerated 'bounce' of sound upon sound communicates the sun's power and another 'incorrigibly plural' scene ('touché, touché'). It makes the poem itself 'A turning page of shine and sound'. MacNeice's more abstract use of internal rhyme has assimilated such effects.

Perhaps, too, emphatic sound reflects his youthful receptivity not only to Ulster's atmospheric sound-track, but to its accents. The 'brangle of talk' ('brangle' is a suitably onomatopoeic dialect word) may count as well as the corncrake. The local voices of Carrickfergus pungently differed from his parents' intonation. MacNeice's friend W. R. Rodgers, a Presbyterian minister from Co. Armagh and later a BBC colleague, himself a poet of onomatopoeic tendencies, characterizes Ulster phonetically in his 'Epilogue' to a book about Ireland they planned together:

> I am Ulster, my people an abrupt people
> Who like the spiky consonants in speech
> And think the soft ones cissy; who dig
> The *k* and *t* in orchestra, detect sin
> In sinfonia, get a kick out of
> Tin cans, fricatives, fornication, staccato talk,
> Anything that gives or takes attack . . .

MacNeice, who retained a slightly grating timbre in his own voice, one adapted to the pronunciation of internal rhymes like 'every evil iron / Siren' ('The Sunlight on the Garden'), often writes of Ulster voices as 'harsh'. The mill-girls' voices were 'harsh and embittered and jeering'; the mother's help 'Miss Craig' '[whose] face was sour and die-hard Puritanical . . . had a rasping Northern accent' (*SAF*, p. 41). Miss Craig's voice contrasts in his memory with the 'music' of his father's 'brogue', and the 'gay warm voice' of Annie, the Catholic cook from rural Tyrone. Yet 'A Personal Digression' in *Zoo* makes some amends to spiky speech:

> The voices of Birmingham are flat, dreary, 'with the salt left out of the soup' as someone said to me. The voices of Belfast are harsh and to an English ear unintelligible, but one feels personality behind them. A harsh personality, but something at least to rely on.

Even MacNeice's dislike of the 'abbreviation Carrick which in the local voice sounded like a slap in the face' pays dividends in the alliterative opening of 'Carrickfergus':

> I was born in Belfast between the mountain and the gantries
> To the hooting of lost sirens and the clang of trams:
> Thence to Smoky Carrick in County Antrim
> Where the bottle-neck harbour collects the mud . . .

The sound sequence 'clang – Smoky Carrick – County – bottle-neck – collects' bears out W. R. Rodgers's point about fricatives. More broadly in the poem, the mutual reinforcement of sense impressions both 'shining' and 'stinking', further reinforced by assonance and alliteration, declares the composite, paradoxical stimulus of MacNeice's local muse: 'Under the peacock aura of a drowning moon'.

It does not matter that we are unable to disentangle the literal from the mythic, the prospective from the retrospective, in MacNeice's accounts of his imaginative cosmos. The subjective and objective components of his imagery are equally inextricable. Church bells, for instance, first made their mark as the sound so regularly heard from the rectory. But this recurrent image also encodes childhood feelings:

> My father being a clergyman, his church was a sort of annex to the home – but rather a haunted annex (it was an old church and there were several things in it which frightened me as a child). Which is one reason, I think, though I would also maintain that the sound is melancholy anyhow, why church bells have for me a sinister association, e.g., in my poem 'Sunday Morning' (*SCLM*, p. 159).

The 'evil bells' of 'An Eclogue for Christmas', by another mutation, begin to sound the social and political alarms of the 1930s. (Similarly, the 'evil iron / Siren' begins as a foghorn and ends as an omen of war.) MacNeice's most affirmative love poem, 'Meeting Point', again twists the image by exploiting its visual aspect. The metallic turns into the organic as love defeats the imperatives of time and duty, together with 'joyless' ghosts from the past:

> The bell was silent in the air
> Holding its inverted poise –
> Between the clang and clang a flower,
> A brazen calyx of no noise:
> The bell was silent in the air.

But, looking back, MacNeice finds few 'moments of glory' to outweigh gloom and omen in his family circumstances: 'guilt, hell fire, Good Friday, the doctor's cough, hurried lamps in the night, melancholia, mongolism, violent sectarian voices . . . sadness and conflict and attrition and frustration' (*SAF*, p. 216). In the poetry, too, actual darkness (lit by too few oil lamps the rectory was full of shadows) coalesces with the shadows cast first by his elder brother's mongolism, then by his mother's melancholia and death. The nursery-rhyme format of 'Autobiography' underlines the origins of nightmare:

> In my childhood trees were green
> And there was plenty to be seen.
>
> *Come back early or never come.*

My father made the walls resound,
He wore his collar the wrong way round.

Come back early or never come.

My mother wore a yellow dress;
Gently, gently, gentleness.

Come back early or never come.

When I was five the black dreams came;
Nothing after was quite the same.

Come back early or never come.

The dark was talking to the dead;
The lamp was dark beside my bed.

Come back early or never come . . .

'Eclogue Between the Motherless' more explicitly probes the condition of motherlessness. The speaker A opens up 'the Bluebeard's closet of the brain', guiltily links his mother's death with his own birth (Mrs MacNeice suffered from a gynaecological illness), and represents himself as

Helpless at the feet of faceless family idols,
Walking the tightrope over the tiger-pit,
Running the gauntlet of inherited fears . . .

B, with a divorce similar to MacNeice's behind him, relates loss of a mother to that of a wife who, after a time of 'heaven come back from the nursery', had become 'scented and alien'. A's question 'can one never find the perfect stranger?' is morbidly answered by his proposal to marry a dying woman. Bereavement conditions the role not only of women and love in MacNeice's poetry, but also of father-figures and religion. Church bells, the 'haunted annex', the dog-collar's 'wrongness', all take colour from the rector's sadness and prayers after his wife's death, and from the inability of prayers to mitigate sadness.

3

Psychoanalysing his early poetry (late 1920s to mid-1930s) in 'Experiences with Images' (*SCLM*, p. 160), MacNeice notes 'images of fear, anxiety, loneliness or monotony'. He sees 'mental illness and mental deficiency' behind 'the *petrifaction* images which appear pretty often in my poems', and cites 'Perseus', a myth tailor-made for him:

> Borrowed wings on his ankles,
> Carrying a stone death,
> The hero entered the hall,
> All in the hall looked up,
> Their breath frozen on them,
> And there was no more shuffle or clatter in the hall at all . . .

He also diagnoses reaction against a 'stone death' in the shape of 'an excessive preoccupation with things dazzling, high-coloured, quick-moving, hedonistic or up-to-date'. 'When We Were Children' recollects the initial attraction of his very medium as colour and dazzle: 'words were coloured . . . And language was a prism'. Thus MacNeice's poetry (like Yeats's) was founded on contraries, on a 'basic conception of life [as] dialectical' (*SCLM*, p. 156). And his dialectic frequently pits darkness against light, petrifaction against flux, puritanism against hedonism.

Light is the inclusive symbolism for all the positives. Being so direct a recoil from darkness – the dark lamp – MacNeice's light intensifies daylight into prismatic light or golden sunlight, the shock of snow-light. The value his poetry attaches to the prism, to a 'peacock aura' or 'conjured inlay on the grass' ('When We Were Children'), originated in the effect of Irish light on his perception:

> An Irish landscape is capable of pantomimic transformation scenes; one moment it will be desolate, dead, unrelieved monotone, the next it will be an indescribably shifting pattern of prismatic light. The light effects of Ireland make other landscapes seem stodgy . . . (*PWBY*, p. 50)

In 'Train to Dublin' (1934) shifting Irish light pervades 'the incidental things' preferred to fixed frameworks of 'idol or idea, creed or king':

> The vivid chequer of the Antrim hills, the trough of dark
> Golden water for the cart-horses, the brass
> Belt of serene sun upon the lough.

Here and elsewhere light is inseparable from the multifaceted sensuous joy in the present which functions as an antidote to 'inherited fears'. Sunlight envelops more of MacNeice's English than Irish landscapes, which retain their physical and psychological option of 'desolate . . . monotone'. This difference has autobiographical roots.

'Woods' (1946) reflects his removal from Carrickfergus to Sherborne in discriminating between Irish and English pastoral. The latter, as countryside, imagery and literary mode, is 'reprieved from the neolithic night / By gamekeepers or by Herrick's girls at play'. 'The Cyclist', written at the same period, condenses life-enhancing summers at Sherborne and Marlborough: 'these five minutes / Are all today and summer'. However, 'freewheeling' will last only 'until the bell/Left-right-left gives his forgotten sentence'. These shades of the Ulster prison-house illustrate how the timeless 'moments of glory' in MacNeice's poetry are accentuated by an ineradicable awareness of their opposite. Once, during the Sherborne school holidays, his brother came home on a visit:

> When he left in a fortnight to return to his Institution I felt a great relief but a guilt that more than balanced it. And the bloom, I felt, had gone off the Dorset hills. And the boys at Sherborne seemed suddenly terribly young; I had learned their language, but they could not learn mine, could never breathe my darkness. (*SAF*, p. 75)

'Mayfly' is the early sunlit poem which stages the fullest confrontation between the forces of life and those of petrifaction:

> Barometer of my moods today, mayfly,
> Up and down one among a million, one
> The same at best as the rest of the jigging mayflies,
> One only day of May alive beneath the sun.
>
> The yokels tilt their pewters and the foam
> Flowers in the sun beside the jewelled water.
> Daughter of the South, call the sunbeams home
> To nest between your breasts. The kingcups
> Ephemeral are gay gulps of laughter.

Gulp of yellow merriment; cackle of ripples;
Lips of the river that pout and whisper round the reeds.
The mayfly flirting and posturing over the water
Goes up and down in the lift so many times for fun.

Published in *Blind Fireworks* and later revised, 'Mayfly' is a love poem to MacNeice's first wife, Mary Ezra ('Mariette' of *The Strings are False*). In 'When I Was Twenty-One' he recalls the impact of this 'Daughter of the South', an exotic and cosmopolitan Jewess: 'a flash of primary colours and a strong waft of chypre . . . superabundant vitality . . . all glitter and bubble and fanfare'. He admits his susceptibility to what 'seemed . . . to be the very opposite of puritanism and a marvellous escape from petit bourgeois mentality'. MacNeice's novel *Roundabout Way* (1932), published under the pseudonym Louis Malone, rebels against this mentality, given a religious tinge by the Reverend Bilbatrox who hails from Ulster. Like 'Snow', 'Mayfly' combats puritanical constrictions in its very fibre and rhythm. As in 'Morning Sun' sunlight not only irradiates but energizes and connects. When the sun goes out, vitality drains from the scene, the gorgon's gaze prevails: 'the streets go cold, the hanging meat / And tiers of fish are colourless and merely dead'. In 'Mayfly' the kingcups, like other yellow flowers in MacNeice's poetry (laburnum, chrysanthemums, dandelions, crocuses), act as a magnet for sunlight. They in turn magnetize the beer ('Flowers'), itself joined by 'foam' to 'the jewelled water', while 'gulp' (visual onomatopoeia) brings in the human element. Different phenomena and sense experiences are once again linked yet distinguished. In 'When I Was Twenty-One' MacNeice remembers himself as 'fascinated not only by D. H. Lawrence but by *The Dance of Life* by Havelock Ellis'. Ellis's 'not original concept of all life as a dance' fed his own longing for 'unity in difference'. (Virginia Woolf also influenced MacNeice's approach to perception, light, time, and the kaleidoscopic flow of experience.) The mayfly who choreographs the poem's vibrant consciousness defies 'solider creeds' with the dance of life.

As a role model for human beings the mayfly is the antithesis of petrifaction. The word 'inconsequent' will recur as a MacNeicean escape hatch because it denies seriality, stony cause and effect, the

Ulster rigidities. The granite sphinxes are in fact an apparition from he 'cemetery beyond the hawthorn hedge': 'Each spring when [Archie the gardener] cut the hedge between the garden and the cemetery a polished granite obelisk would reappear looking over at us' (*SAF*, p. 48). Whereas the sphinxes denote petrified philosophies, as well as other forms of death, the mayflies' 'dance above the dazzling wave' symbolizes man's ideally fluid relation to a fluid universe. It constitutes MacNeice's most elaborate early answer to the problem of creed in an unsolid world. The answer involves more than a recommendation to gather kingcups while ye may. The fusion of light with water establishes a fertile concept and emblem of flux embraced as a positive condition, the condition of being fully alive. ('River in Spate' puts the dialectically opposite proposition.) Flux, both as a state of affairs and a state of consciousness, maximizes the movement intrinsic to life. Such 'elasticity' steals time's own weapons: 'what of time they have / They stretch out taut and thin and ringing clear'. 'Ringing clear' implies the poet's own role in animating the scene. In the last stanza love, life, and the power of creative mind over inert matter counter fatality:

> It is we who pass them, we the circus masters
> Who make the mayflies dance, the lapwings lift their crests,
> The show will soon shut down, its gay-rags gone,
> But when this summer is over let us die together,
> I want always to be near your breasts.

'Show' is no mere afterthought or surface theatricality. MacNeice's metaphors of life as performance integrate his modes of highlighting, of antithesis to the dead dumbshow of granite sphinxes.

The conflict takes various forms in other early lyrics. Some, like 'Snow', 'Morning Sun' and 'Mayfly', comment on their own aesthetics, on the artist's problem of doing justice to flux within his own patterns. 'Train to Dublin' stresses variousness and flux ('the faces balanced in the toppling wave') by refusing 'further syntheses', both philosophical and artistic. 'August' and 'Nature Morte' find more difficulty in assuming that the mind can 'follow / The living curve that is breathlessly the same'. Both poems reflect the interest in the visual arts which dates from MacNeice's friendship with Anthony Blunt at Marlborough, and which may also tint his 'jewelled' colours. 'August', wrestling with the paradox of 'still life', finds the poet's as well as the painter's solution inadequate: 'I, like Poussin, make a still-bound fête of us / Suspending every noise, of insect or machine'. The conclusion lacks the creative confidence of 'Mayfly', while drawing a similar moral: 'Our mind, being dead, wishes to have time die'. 'Nature Morte', on the other hand, detects life in still life but at the cost of catharsis: 'And in your Chardin the appalling unrest of the soul / Exudes from the dried fish and the brown jug and the bowl'. 'The Glacier' strikes a balance between unrest and arrest by again attaching a measure of control to the mind's eye. The first part of the poem plays a game with time and perception which causes flux to become indistinguishable from petrifaction. A 'quick motion film' of traffic, days, and years slows into a 'catafalque'. Yet, by averting our gaze to 'seemingly slower things', we may find real movement in creative particulars as opposed to life's general, funeral course. The poem ends by celebrating a scholar's mental 'speed of fins and wings' and an old gardener's (Archie's) services to 'the roaring sap of vegetables'.

Changes of stance and angle are essential to MacNeice's developing dialectic. This of course also operates less abstractly and more dramatically. Individual protagonists seem poised between the fear and joy of life, between the promptings of negative and affirmative voices. 'Happy Families', a different kind of still life, satirizes 'petit bourgeois' existence as petrifaction: 'Crusted in sandstone . . . We seem fossils in rock, / Or leaves turned mummies in drouth.' The voice of convention ('Nobody disgraced us, luckily for us') shuts out the voice of the wind who

> Raps at front door, back door, side door;
> In spite of the neat placard that says
> 'NO HAWKERS HERE' he knocks the more . . .

In 'Spring Voices' the sun 'shouts cheerily' as part of another ironically insistent campaign mounted by the life force, and underscored by noise. The voice of caution, on the other hand, sounds a warning about life's dangers that echoes from MacNeice's childhood: 'Keep the wind out, cast no clout, try no unwarranted jaunts untried before'. In 'Sunday Morning' the poem's own voice challenges the dictates of 'skulls' mouths'. 'An April Manifesto' even more didactically asserts human rights to frivolity, to 'Sharp sun-strop, surface-gloss, and momentary caprice'. MacNeice's peculiarly exhilarated sense of spring once again reacts against a metaphorical 'vigil in the wintry chapel'. Thus 'surface-gloss' marks a deep relish nurtured by darkness. The conclusion of 'An Eclogue for Christmas', contemporary with these lyrics, confirms the overall thrust of MacNeice's early poetry towards music, movement, and sensuous and mental vitality, whatever the risks and shadows:

A. Let the saxophones and the xylophones
And the cult of every technical excellence, the miles of canvas in the galleries
And the canvas of the rich man's yacht snapping and tacking on the seas
And the perfection of a grilled steak –
B. Let all these so ephemeral things
Be somehow permanent like the swallow's tangent wings:
Goodbye to you, this day remember is Christmas, this morn
They say, interpret it your own way, Christ is born.

In so interpreting the Christmas message, MacNeice certainly rewrites voices and orthodoxies of his childhood.

4

'Darkest Ulster', of course, is not only a personal or subjective matter:

And I remember, when I was little, the fear
Bandied among the servants
That Casement would land at the pier
With a sword and a horde of rebels;
And how we used to expect, at a later date,
When the wind blew from the west, the noise of shooting
Starting in the evening at eight
In Belfast in the York Street district;

And the voodoo of the Orange bands
  Drawing an iron net through darkest Ulster,
Flailing the limbo lands . . .

(*Autumn Journal* XVI)

The politics of MacNeice's Irish poems begin in childhood because Irish politics begin with the family and not at voting age. Hence the deeper sedimentation of his political awareness than was usual among English writers during the 1930s. Even if his memoirs overstylize the rectory 'servants', he undoubtedly absorbed Ulster cross-currents from Miss Craig and Annie, both of whom enriched his poetry's folk-lore (Miss Craig's tales of will o' the wisps sparked off an image in 'Elegy for Minor Poets' and Annie first asked 'The Riddle'). Archie added further folk-lore, and proof that an individual Orangeman might lack the mass vices. 'The Gardener' in 'Novelettes' is the most unclouded poem to recall Carrickfergus. The following stanza shows the acceptable face of religious Ulster:

He believed in God –
The Good Fellow Up There –
And he used a simile of Homer
Watching the falling leaves,
And every year he waited for the Twelfth of July,
Cherishing his sash and his fife
For the carnival of banners and drums.
He was always claiming but never
Obtaining his old age pension,
For he did not know his age.

MacNeice lovingly dispatches Archie 'in a trim boat / To find the Walls of Derry / Or the land of the Ever Young'. This Nirvana unites Celtic mythology (Tír-na-nÓg) with Ulster Protestant mythology (the siege of Derry).

But in 'Carrickfergus' the historical and social location of MacNeice's family epitomizes disunity:

The Norman walled his town against the country
  To stop his ears to the yelping of his slave

And built a church in the form of a cross but denoting
The list of Christ on the cross in the angle of the nave.

I was the rector's son, born to the anglican order,
Banned for ever from the candles of the Irish poor;
The Chichesters knelt in marble at the end of a transept
With ruffs about their necks, their portion sure.

The war came and a huge camp of soldiers
Grew from the ground in sight of our house with long
Dummies hanging from gibbets for bayonet practice
And the sentry's challenge echoing all day long;

A Yorkshire terrier ran in and out by the gate-lodge
Barred to civilians, yapping as if taking affront:
Marching at ease and singing 'Who Killed Cock Robin?'
The troops went out by the lodge and off to the Front.

These quatrains cover oppression and war in Ulster from the Normans, to dynasties like the Chichesters (a Major Chichester-Clark was Stormont Prime Minister in the early 1970s), to the First World War. The contrast between the Scotch and Irish Quarters of Carrickfergus has already registered the continuing inequality and division produced by past invasions, including the largely Scottish plantation of Ulster in the early seventeenth century. The chorus of noise ('yelping – echoing – yapping – singing') signifies social as well as personal disturbance, and the poem accumulates images of siege and barriers: 'bottle-neck – walled – banned – barred'; later, 'a prison ship for Germans, / A cage across their sight'. The poem's own sensory alertness is at odds with people who deny others or themselves (the Norman 'stopping his ears') the full use of their senses. The images of murder and maiming, too, obviously go beyond one child's 'black dreams'. It is appropriate that the church of St Nicholas – 'listing' on several counts perhaps – should be a focus for history and politics. 'Born to the anglican order', a phrase which may pun on British rule, signifies membership of the once-established (Anglican) Church of Ireland, and thus distance from Roman Catholics on the one hand, and to a lesser extent from Presbyterians (the Scotch Quarter) on the other. MacNeice's attribution of hell-fire theology to Miss Craig (see discussion of 'The Blasphemies', page 141) shows that he at least sniffed the brimstone of sterner creeds than his father's. John Frederick MacNeice's career illustrates the point that: 'Religion in Ireland is . . . still inextricably fused with social life and politics' (*Zoo*). He was in fact an untypical Protestant clergyman. In 1912 he refused to sign the Covenant against Irish Home Rule. Later, as Bishop of Down, Connor and Dromore, he 'scandalized Belfast' because he 'refused to allow the Union Jack to be hung over Carson's tomb in perpetuity' (*Zoo*). In the mid-1930s Bishop MacNeice campaigned against the sectarian violence of that time. In *Letters from Iceland* (1937) his son praises him for '[fixing] / His pulpit out of the reach of party slogans' ('Last Will and Testament' by MacNeice and Auden).

MacNeice's own critiques of Ireland also resist party slogans. In 'Eclogue from Iceland' 'Ryan' explains his 'exile' as follows:

> I come from an island, Ireland, a nation
> Built upon violence and morose vendettas.
> My diehard countrymen like drayhorses
> Drag their ruin behind them.
> Shooting straight in the cause of crooked thinking
> Their greed is sugared with pretence of public spirit.
> From all which I am an exile.

Other poems which contain explicit socio-political comment on Ireland are: 'Belfast' (1931), 'Valediction' (1934), *Autumn Journal* XVI (1938), 'The Closing Album' (1939) and 'Neutrality' (written during the Second World War). That chronology coincides with the period when MacNeice's poetry in general was most exercised about public issues. Even the Ireland of 'Carrickfergus' also belongs to a wider British and European context, to a time of new wars mapped by 'flags on pins moving across and across'.

MacNeice perceives certains sins as common to the whole of Ireland: slogans, 'violence and morose vendettas', obsession with history, parochial introversion, 'grandiose airs' – in fact all-round petrifaction. His personae escape self-righteousness by internalizing some of the above as their own failings: 'a gesture and a brogue / And a faggot of useless memories' (*Autumn Journal*).

However, he also distinguishes between Northern and Southern manifestations of the national faults. Thus his poetry calls the North 'hard' and the South 'soft', even though these categories gradually became more complicated: 'as with Belfast it took me years to penetrate its outer ugliness and dourness, so with Dublin it took me years to see through its soft charm to its bitter prickly kernel – which I quite like too' (*SAF*, p. 222). 'Belfast' is another case of consonantal sound returning to the environment which produced it:

> The hard cold fire of the northerner
> Frozen into his blood from the fire in his basalt
> Glares from behind the mica of his eyes
> And the salt carrion water brings him wealth.
>
> Down there at the end of the melancholy lough
> Against the lurid sky over the stained water
> Where hammers clang murderously on the girders
> Like crucifixes the gantries stand.

Verbal hammering sets up a scenario of violence and victimization. 'Like crucifixes the gantries stand' brilliantly fuses industrial and religious oppressiveness, to symbolize Protestant rule. A 'shawled factory-woman', prostrated 'before the garish Virgin', personifies the suffering inflicted by a comprehensively brutal ethos characterized as masculine: 'the male kind murders each its woman'. The middle quatrain, which attacks merely commercial exploitation ('harsh / Attempts at buyable beauty'), seems literally out of place, imported from the less 'lurid' world of 'Birmingham' (1933). 'Valediction' again lists 'hard' images of Belfast and any redeeming Ulster features, such as 'water-shafted air / Of amethyst and moonstone', come from elsewhere.

Later in the 1930s the 'Personal Digression' in *Zoo* modified MacNeice's imagery of the hard city itself:

> The weekend was all sunshine. I could not remember Belfast like this, and the continuous sunshine delighted but outraged me. My conception of Belfast, built up since early childhood, demanded that it should always be grey, wet, repellent and its inhabitants dour, rude and callous . . .

> My family's house lay under the Black Mountain – not black, but a luminous grey-blue. There was no speck of wetness on the streets. The macabre elements seemed to have vanished – no El Greco faces under shawls, no torn feet or newsboys leaping on racing trams . . .
>
> It was very possible that Ulstermen were bigots, sadists, witch-doctors, morons. I had seen their Twelfths of July. But I had always dramatized them into the Enemy. They were not really grandiose monsters. If they were lost, they were lost with a small 'l'.

The account of the North in *Autumn Journal* is all the more powerful for being less impressionistic, and less subjectively melodramatic, than MacNeice's previous versions. Ominous sound ('the noise of shooting . . . And the voodoo of the Orange bands') now heralds specific economic, social and political analysis:

> And the North, where I was a boy,
> Is still the North, veneered with the grime of Glasgow,
> Thousands of men whom nobody will employ
> Standing at the corners, coughing.
> And the street-children play on the wet
> Pavement – hopscotch or marbles;
> And each rich family boasts a sagging tennis-net
> On a spongy lawn beside a dripping shrubbery.
> The smoking chimneys hint
> At prosperity round the corner
> But they make their Ulster linen from foreign lint
> And the money that comes in goes out to make more money.
> A city built upon mud;
> A culture built upon profit;
> Free speech nipped in the bud,
> The minority always guilty.

That indictment summarizes unemployment, inequality, an off-shore economy, irresponsible capitalism, injustice and repression. MacNeice's analysis also emphasizes the gulf between 'minority' and majority in other ways. 'Ode' (1934), a poem about his newborn son on the lines of Yeats's 'A Prayer for my Daughter', had already questioned Irish Nationalist assumptions about unity: 'chewing the old lie / That parallel lines will meet at infinity'. *Autumn Journal* XVI includes a related metaphor of polarization, one which still defines the Ulster conflict:

And one read black where the other read white, his hope
   The other man's damnation:
Up the Rebels, To Hell with the Pope,
   And God Save – as you prefer – the King or Ireland.

If MacNeice's images and definitions apply today, it is not only because Northern Ireland has not changed much, but because insights endure. Like his father, he always remained sympathetic to the concept of a united Ireland. Indeed his poetry unifies the country *de facto* by its panoramic method, its reiteration of shared sins. However, by the early 1930s some of the dreams which had assisted at the birth in 1922 of the Irish Free State had evaporated. 'A Prayer for my Daughter' (1919), also about national birth-pangs, incorporates 'great gloom'. Yeats's gloom since 1916 was partly occasioned by the burning of 'big houses' owned by the Anglo-Irish gentry. The burnings continued and led to a considerable exodus of Southern Irish Protestants. 'Valediction' advises: 'Admire the suavity with which the architect / Is rebuilding the burnt mansion'. Protestant writers and intellectuals who had promoted the Nationalist cause were particularly prone to disillusionment. They worried about the power of the Catholic Church in the new state, and about official insistence on a 'Gaelic' cultural ambience sometimes antagonistic to Irish literature in English as exemplified by the Irish Literary Revival. Yeats when a senator fought against the prevailing wind on issues such as divorce. From 1929 writers of all backgrounds were united against censorship. In his autobiography *Missing Persons* E. R. Dodds, who knew Yeats and other figures of the Revival, gives representative reasons for becoming 'a permanent *émigré*': 'I and the intellectual group to which I belonged were coming to feel like foreign bodies in this outwardly Gaelicized but at heart increasingly philistine Ireland which tolerated us but felt no need for our services.'

'Valediction' and MacNeice's unpublished political farce

Station Bell (written c.1935 for the Birmingham University Dramatic Society) inhabit this zone of feeling. *Station Bell* conceives what William T. McKinnon calls 'a peculiar brand of Irish Fascism' (*Apollo's Blended Dream*). The proposals of Julia Brown, 'a lady Hitler', for a Propaganda Corps suggest MacNeice's view of the existing state ideology: 'Such a corps will be both official and informal, betokening the spontaneity of our movement, a body of men and women of typically national appearance symbolizing the new Ireland which is superseding the old, but is yet the consummation of what was good in the old.' Julia eventually advances her dominance by scapegoating Communism as the national enemy. It should be remembered that conservative, clerical Ireland had become especially unattractive to anyone of left-wing inclinations. 'Eclogue from Iceland' mentions as a hero '[James] Connolly / Vilified now by the gangs of Catholic Action'. 'Valediction' criticizes the national dream (incorporating MacNeice's dream of Ireland) as a God that failed. Words like 'fake', 'glamour', 'sham', 'trick', 'fantasy' emphasize discrepancies between propaganda or façade and actuality. So do factual reminders of emigration and of violence: 'minds / Fuddled with blood'. The latter embraces the North; but the South stands more heavily accused of inner discrepancy, of the self-deception that swallows home-made propaganda as MacNeice has swallowed his own manufactures: 'Take credit for our sanctity, our heroism and our sterile want'. *Autumn Journal* XVI, with greater rhetorical precision, similarly punctures clichés of the national self-image:

The land of scholars and saints:
  Scholars and saints my eye, the land of ambush,
Purblind manifestoes, never-ending complaints . . .

The bombs in the turnip sack, the sniper from the roof,
  Griffith, Connolly, Collins, where have they brought us?
Ourselves alone! Let the round tower stand aloof
  In a world of bursting mortar!
Let the school-children fumble their sums
  In a half-dead language;

Let the censor be busy on the books; pull down the Georgian slums;
 Let the games be played in Gaelic.
Let them grow beet-sugar; let them build
 A factory in every hamlet;
Let them pigeon-hole the souls of the killed
 Into sheep and goats, patriots and traitors.

As with the North, the Free State's sins are now more specific to its social and ideological organization: censorship, doctrinaire Gaelicization, environmental vandalism, selective sympathy for 'the souls of the killed' after the Civil War which followed Independence. This second valediction has much in common with its predecessor, including 'Memory in apostasy', the itemizing structure of a balance sheet or law trial, and the mode of 'overstatement' (see MacNeice's note to *Autumn Journal*) or satirical excess. However, not only is '*Odi atque amo*' more thoroughly internalized and conceptualized, it takes its place within a larger awareness. The country as a whole embodies some of the political morals that *Autumn Journal* draws from the Munich crisis. As propaganda and censorship, Ireland symbolizes partisan corruptions of language. As an unrealized Utopia, it symbolizes the collapse of other political dreams. As a self-deceiving, introverted island, it symbolizes insulation against the meaning of Munich: 'Let the round tower stand aloof / In a world of bursting mortar!' And as a breeder of fanatical loyalties, it clarifies the priorities of the liberal incapable of the committed 'single purpose' Autumn 1938 seems to demand:

 We envy men of action
Who sleep and wake, murder and intrigue
 Without being doubtful, without being haunted.
And I envy the intransigence of my own
 Countrymen who shoot to kill and never
See the victim's face become their own
 Or find his motive sabotage their motives.

Written less than a year later, 'The Closing Album' proves the continuing plasticity of MacNeice's Ireland. Originally longer and called 'The Coming of War', this sequence is based on a late-summer holiday in 1939, a holiday taken after 'the fatalist within me' had said: 'War or no war, you have got to go back to the West. If only for a week. Because you may never again' (*SAF*, p. 210). In addition to 'Sligo and Mayo' (III) and 'Galway' (IV) the sequence includes 'Dublin' (I), 'Cushendun' (II) – a village in the Glens of Antrim – and a fifth untitled poem. On the one hand, the album commemorates Irish light and other sense impressions as the pleasures of flux and peace: 'a welter of nasturtium / Deluging the sight'. On the other, the map of Ireland too is shaded by questions ultimately put in the poem which lacks geographical attachment:

> And why should the sea maintain its turbulence, its elegance,
> And draw a film of muslin down the sand
> With each receding wave?
>
> And why, now it has happened,
> Should the atlas still be full of the maps of countries
> We never shall see again?

By holding Irish and European horizons in the same frame, MacNeice dramatizes a consciousness grappling with change: 'What a place to talk of War'. Thus Sligo flickers from milkmaid pastoral ('little distant fields were sprigged with haycocks') to less Arcadian prospects whereby the first of MacNeice's dream worlds supplies his last thirties omens:

> And pullets pecking the flies from around the eyes of heifers
>   Sitting in farmyard mud
> Among hydrangeas and the falling ear-rings
>   Of fuchsias red as blood.

'Cushendun' is short of main verbs. 'Galway' has a definitive statement as its refrain: 'The war came down on us here.' In between, 'Sligo and Mayo' concentrates the overall dynamic by letting images speak for themselves.

Ireland's likely neutrality during the war contributes to the sequence's atmosphere of being in two worlds at once. Later, the poem actually called 'Neutrality' was to take a political and hostile view of this policy as a further instance of the round tower standing aloof, of navel-gazing into the past at the expense of the present:

Look into your heart, you will find a County Sligo,
A Knocknarea with for navel a cairn of stones,
You will find the shadow and sheen of a moleskin mountain
And a litter of chronicles and bones . . .

But then look eastward from your heart, there bulks
A continent, close, dark, as archetypal sin,
While to the west off your own shores the mackerel
Are fat – on the flesh of your kin.

However, the earlier 'Dublin' should perhaps be regarded as MacNeice's 'balanced' version of where his poetry stands in relation to Irish national culture and politics. 'Dublin' 'poises the toppling hour' before more shaken and open-ended poems take over the sequence. It does so by conflating MacNeice's ambivalence about Ireland with the perplexities of the time, and with the role of this ambivalence in shaping his whole sensibility. Discrepancies between façades and interior reality are resolved within a wider charity that also admits an attraction to such antinomies: 'The glamour of her squalor, / The bravado of her talk'. Nevertheless, deceptive 'softness' remains exposed for what it is:

But oh the days are soft,
Soft enough to forget
The lesson better learnt,
The bullet on the wet
Streets, the crooked deal,
The steel behind the laugh,
The Four Courts burnt.

Here and in the previous stanza Ireland's two-facedness again insinuates the sly proximity of peace and war:

And the mist on the Wicklow hills
Is close, as close
As the peasantry were to the landlord,
As the Irish to the Anglo-Irish,
As the killer is close one moment
To the man he kills . . .

The concluding imagery and rhythm, by fusing the architectural with the organic, reconcile natural and man-made Ireland, '*Odi atque amo*':

> Fort of the Dane,
> Garrison of the Saxon,
> Augustan capital
> Of a Gaelic nation,
> Appropriating all
> The alien brought,
> You give me time for thought
> And by a juggler's trick
> You poise the toppling hour –
> O greyness run to flower,
> Grey stone, grey water,
> And brick upon grey brick.

Further, although 'she will not / Have me alive or dead' has already discounted even MacNeice's literary reputation in the city, Dublin's mongrel genealogy resembles his own. On the whole he enjoyed rather than lamented the contradictions of his pedigree: 'Speaking as an Irishman of Southern blood and Northern upbringing, whose father was a Protestant Bishop and also a fervent Home Ruler . . .' (review of Honor Tracy's book about Ireland, *Mind You, I've Said Nothing*). As Dublin lends itself to appropriation by a kindred alien – 'She is not an Irish town / And she is not English' – the poem comes to terms with Irish history, with MacNeice's own implication in that history, and with its implications for him. Dublin's power to 'hold [his] mind' suggests the extent to which Ireland has conditioned the dialectical structure of his imagination.

5

The poems discussed above also indicate that MacNeice's poetry has an Irish, as well as an English, *literary* context. Several of them maintain an implicit dialogue with Yeats, whether by revising his landscapes or by redefining the Yeatsian 'man of action'. (Chapter V examines some aesthetic aspects of this dialogue.) MacNeice's consciousness of Yeats, indeed, bridges his own double context: not only Yeats's significance for twentieth-century poetry in general, but for Irish poetry in particular, and for MacNeice's own relation to both traditions. Despite his different brand of 'Anglo-Irish' hybridization, his half-way house between the conditions of Anglo-Irishman and Ulster Protestant, MacNeice is the major Irish poet after Yeats who follows him in broad cultural orientation. Hence perhaps his suggestion in *The Poetry of W. B. Yeats* that Yeats's posterity within Ireland did not satisfy Yeats himself:

> Most of his Irish successors followed him in eschewing the industrial world and in writing their verses carefully, but they followed him in little else. There is rarely much meat on their poems. Yeats himself seems at times to have felt impatient with them, to have turned away towards English poets who were breaking his own rules. (pp. 179–80)

On the other island MacNeice now inclines to 'group' the thirties school of poets 'with Yeats rather than with Eliot'. In any case, an autobiographical 'Irish Background' chapter exemplifies the inevitability of his engaging with Yeats on more levels than did Auden:

> When I read Yeats's account of his childhood I find many things which are echoed in my own or in that of other Irish people I know – in particular, the effects of loneliness or a primitive rural life; the clannish obsession with one's own family; the combination of an anarchistic individualism with puritanical taboos and inhibitions . . . the constant desire to show off . . . (p. 52)

One mythic 'echo' is the West of Ireland. Since Yeats in the 1880s was first 'haunted by numberless islands . . . / Where Time would surely forget us, and Sorrow come near us no more' ('The White Birds'), the West has borne symbolic and transcendental meanings in the work of Irish Protestant writers. As MacNeice puts it in 'Western Landscape': 'The west of Ireland / Is brute and ghost at once'. In his essay 'Certain Set Apart' (see *Fictions of the*

Irish Literary Revival, 1987) John Wilson Foster analyses the *national* meaning of the West:

> the Irish cultural renaissance involved a new version of island mythology, a creation myth for an imminent new order. The western island . . . came to represent Ireland's mythic unity before the Chaos of conquest: there at once were the vestige and the symbolic entirety of an undivided nation.

For Protestant writers, gradually less certain than their Catholic counterparts as to whether the 'new order' wanted them, the West additionally came to express oblique territorial claims, intangible rights in the country. Relatively unpopulated (whether island or mainland), it could represent, besides primordial unity, a clean slate where old conflicts might be resolved and new definitions founded. In 'Eclogue from Iceland' Ryan's anti-Utopian Ireland is set against Grettir's (and MacNeice's) ideal:

> There is only hope for people who live upon islands
> Where the Lowest Common labels will not stick
> And the unpolluted hills will hold your echo.

The landscape's beauty helped to translate political issues on to a less contentious plane, to define Utopia in terms of Hy Brasil. This paralleled MacNeice's general creative trajectory in the post-war period. Earlier, the dismissive allusion in 'Neutrality' to Yeats's Sligo also covered the fact that Sligo is another western ancestral home of the MacNeice family. Thus the poem enjoins its author, as well as Ireland, to resist the mythic backward look, the lure of western seas now polluted by U-boats. From 1945 onwards, however, as public events receded and his poetry turned to parabolic approaches, the West replaced the body politic of North or South at the centre of MacNeice's direct imaginative contact with Ireland.

This was of course partly due to his now having become irrevocably 'one of your holiday visitors', as 'Valediction' threatens. 'Western Landscape', an *ave* ten years on to complement that farewell, distils the essence both of holiday visits and the West's appeal:

In doggerel and stout let me honour this country
Though the air is so soft that it smudges the words . . .
For the western climate is Lethe,
The smoky taste of cooking on turf is lotus,
There are affirmation and abnegation together
From the broken bog with its veins of amber water,
From the distant headland, a sphinx's fist, that barely grips the
  sea . . .

'Softness' and amnesia reappear, but without the moral backlash of 'Dublin' or 'Neutrality'. The association of the West with Lethe, lotus, and later a siren's song recalls Yeats's timeless islands, 'The Wanderings of Oisin'. However, a less escapist wanderer personifies MacNeice's feeling for the West as a surrogate, not for the nation, but for religion:

O Brandan, spindrift hermit, who
Hankering roaming un-homing up-anchoring
From this rock wall looked seawards to
Knot the horizon round your waist,
Distil that distance and undo
Time in quintessential West . . .

MacNeice was always attracted to the ninth-century *Navigatio* of St Brendan (or Brandan) in which the Saint sets forth in a stone boat on a western voyage of faith. His radio play *The Mad Islands* (1962) reworks another ninth-century voyage tale, the Gaelic *Immram Mael Duin*. Both Mael Duin's circumnavigation of strange 'otherworld' islands and Brendan's quest for 'quintessential West' have a diffused influence on MacNeice's later parables. In 'Western Landscape' he characteristically renders Brendan's epiphany in terms of its ocean context, and as a fusion of physical and mental consciousness:

One thought of God, one feeling of the ocean,
Fused in the moving body, the unmoved soul,
Made him a part of a not to be parted whole.
Whole.
And the West was all the world, the lonely was the only,

The chosen – and there was no choice – the Best,
For the beyond was here . . .

But integrated visions seem a purely spiritual possibility. At the end of the poem genetic and political language excludes 'the visitor':

Let now the visitor, although disfranchised
In the constituencies of quartz and bog-oak
And ousted from the elemental congress,
. . .
let me, if a bastard
Out of the West by urban civilization
(Which unwished father claims me – so I must take
What I can before I go) let me who am neither Brandan
Free of all roots nor yet a rooted peasant
Here add one stone to the indifferent cairn . . .

Although this implies factors excluding MacNeice from Ireland as a 'whole', the uprooted state of being 'a bastard / Out of the West by urban civilization' is also a representative modern condition (one that increasingly applies to Ireland itself). In the late 1930s MacNeice's version of a related western landscape had been explicitly social, if numinously fringed. 'The Hebrides' (1937) reacts against 'semaphore ultimatums tick by tick' by relishing an island Utopia full of natural balances: Here 'The tethered cow grazes among the orchises'. This model community, where 'the art of being a stranger with your neighbour / Has still to be imported', elaborates Grettir's 'hope'. It resembles, too, MacNeice's quickly banished notion of Ireland in *Autumn Journal*: 'that on this tiny stage with luck a man / Might see the end of one particular action.' However, 'The Hebrides' does not ignore the economic, cultural, and political tides threatening a traditional way of life, which also carries seeds of its own destruction: 'many live on the dole or on old-age pensions / And many waste with consumption and some are drowned'. The end of the poem can promise only: 'There is still peace though not for me and not / Perhaps for long . . .'

'The beyond' and Utopia remain elusive goals on MacNeice's western horizons. His West is a state of yearning rather than of fulfilment: a means of questing. Thus 'Last before America' terms the legendary Atlantic island Hy Brasil

> an image
> For those who despise charts but find their dream's endorsement
> In certain long low islets snouting towards the west
> Like cubs that have lost their mother.

The poet who lost his own western mother identifies with the seeking islets. In the mid-1940s and mid-1950s MacNeice wrote groups of poems in which western landscapes function as a topography for metaphysical inquiry. The human presence faces problems of orientation amid a relativistic flux of space and time. The first group, based on a visit to Achill Island in 1945, includes 'Littoral', 'The Strand', 'Last before America', 'Under the Mountain', and 'No More Sea'. The poems hinge on conflicting perspectives: the godlike view from the mountain-top and the 'wrack' below sizzling 'with stinking life'; longings to emigrate followed by the reminder that 'the travellers died the same / As those who stayed in Ireland'. 'The Strand' is a 'mirror of wet sand' which enables the poet to capture and commemorate his father: 'A square black figure whom the horizon understood'. But this understanding, paid-up membership of 'the elemental congress', offers no solidity either amid a ceaseless fluctuation which erases marks of the human body and mind:

> Sixty-odd years behind him and twelve before,
> Eyeing the flange of steel in the turning belt of brine
> It was sixteen years ago he walked this shore
>
> And the mirror caught his shape which catches mine
> But then as now the floor-mop of the foam
> Blotted the bright reflections – and no sign
>
> Remains of face or feet when visitors have gone home.

The later sequence 'A Hand of Snapshots', as the titles indicate, concerns similar comings and goings: 'The Left-Behind', 'The Back-Again', 'The Gone-Tomorrow', 'The Once-in-Passing', 'The Here-and-Never'. All but the first of these titles might personify MacNeice's own relation to Ireland. At the same time, they illustrate the complex perception developed by the uncertainties of this relation. 'A Hand of Snapshots' uses the lenses of multiple perceivers in place of the pictorial double focus of 'The Closing Album'. The poems symbolize a spectrum of earthly longings and belongings by presenting the impact of the West as ranging from the ironically rendered saturation of 'The Left-Behind' immobilized by 'a past of lazybeds' ('lazybeds' are the marks of former potato-fields abandoned due to famine or emigration), to the brief attention-span of 'The Gone-Tomorrow' – a holidaying child who will forget 'mottled fields and marbled foam'. 'The Here-and-Never' extracts a Utopian vision from all this flux, one which combines flesh and spirit, the positives of rooted living and of mobile consciousness:

> Here it was living and dying, but never
> Lifelong dying or dead-alive.
> Few were few but all knew all,
> The all were few and therefore many,
> Landscape and seascape at one's call,
> The senses five or more than five.

Earlier, 'No More Sea' had also restored Brendan's epiphany to the world. A social parable for the 1940s, the poem contrasts an 'age of mainlanders, that dare not fancy / Life out of uniform' with the responsively dynamic existence of 'islanders whose hearts themselves are islands', with

> what it meant to live embroiled with ocean
> And between moving dunes and beyond reproving
> Sentry-boxes to have been self-moving.

The projection of the island as both self and sea is a pointer to the ideal 'anarchic democracy' always 'round the corner'.

MacNeice has undoubtedly taken the western island well beyond its roles in the Irish Literary Revival. Yet perhaps his interest in the myth always repeats one original starting-point of Yeats and Synge. John Wilson Foster notes that 'the western island was [also] for the writers a potent symbol of the self's isolation'. 'Donegal Triptych', which precedes 'A Hand of Snapshots', seems to conflate this with an idea MacNeice took over from the Marxist poet and critic Christopher Caudwell ('the instinctive ego of art is the common man into which we retire to establish contact with our fellows'):

So now from this heathered and weathered perch I watch the grey
  waves pucker
And feel the hand of the wind on my throat again,
Once more having entered solitude once more to find communion
With other solitary beings, with the whole race of men.

MacNeice's efforts to reconcile 'solitude' and 'communion' (the 'union in solitude' of 'Round the Corner'), whether socially or spiritually directed, derive in part from his loss of the fixed cultural-religious co-ordinates which still place a majority of his countrymen. But personal loss can be artistic opportunity, as already suggested, and as 'The Once-in-Passing' may hint. This self-dramatization dashes dreams of the alternative life MacNeice might have lived in the West of Ireland, perhaps as the Catholic peasant he (erroneously) supposed to be among his forebears:

And here the cross on the window means myself
But that window does not open;
Born here, I should have proved a different self.
Such vistas dare not open;
For what can walk or talk without tongue or feet?

Nevertheless, by virtue of 'imagination' as well as honesty, the poem finally negotiates a tentative link between MacNeice's actual autobiography and the emblem of a corporate Christian Irish past. The conclusion echoes 'An Eclogue for Christmas' in attaching new possibility to old 'vistas':

Yet here for a month, and for this once in passing,
I can imagine at least
The permanence of what passes,
As though the window opened
And the ancient cross on the hillside meant myself.

That communion, like the geology of 'Carrick Revisited', gives the poet a stake in the country and the country a stake in the poetry.

II
English Choices

I

England of the 1930s complemented MacNeice's Irish background, just as the very different England of the 1890s had complemented Yeats's. When MacNeice summarizes the role of the nineties aesthetic movement in Yeats's career, he might be describing his own relation to other 'thirties poets': '[He] was at the same time of them and not of them; some of their doctrine persisted in his mind to the end but always he applied it his own way' (*PWBY*, p. 32). MacNeice skipped certain thirties literary rites of passage. He did not become a disciple of Auden's at Oxford; he was not represented in the epoch-making anthologies *New Signatures* (1932) and *New Country* (1933); he did not join the Communist Party; and, unlike Christopher Isherwood and others, he did not visit Weimar Berlin, as 'When I Was Twenty-One' confesses: 'I often wonder what difference it would have made to me if I had had a Berlin to say goodbye to.' On the other hand, he later forged a closer poetic alliance with Auden as a result of living in Birmingham (Auden's home city), an alliance ratified by their tour of Iceland in 1936 and joint publication of *Letters from Iceland* (1937). In addition, MacNeice was a pillar of *New Verse* and of Rupert Doone's Group Theatre; he did go (twice) to Spain; and he wrote the poem which is in several senses the last word on the decade – *Autumn Journal* (1939). But if by autumn 1938 MacNeice was expressing the Zeitgeist more comprehensively than Auden, his perspectives still owe something to the distance of an outsider. Francis Scarfe in *Auden and After* takes an Anglo-centric view when he regrets MacNeice's lack of 'one of Auden's stabilizing qualities, his understanding and love of England'. But Anglo-Irish double vision, often as little noticed in England as appreciated in Ireland, gains in critical insight for not being wholly affiliated to either country:

But I have also this other, this English, choice
Into what yet is foreign . . .
('Woods')

As Samuel Hynes demonstrates in *The Auden Generation*, the 1930s are not just another literary period, but also a cultural myth which the writers themselves constructed. This myth, still perpetuating and revising itself, hinges on relations between literature and politics. However, it belongs much more emphatically to the history of the former than of the latter. Robin Skelton comments in his introduction to *Poetry of the Thirties*:

> [The poets] talked in an almost empty theatre as if it were a packed Wembley Stadium. They argued, proved, disproved, and judged, as if the whole nation were listening. They had, in fact, discovered a drama and invented an audience.

The talk really got underway with the publication of Auden's *Poems* (1930) and with Michael Roberts's codification in his introduction to *New Signatures* – stressing 'solidarity with others' and the intellectual's duty to 'lead'. There was certainly solidarity with regard to the literary leadership of W. H. Auden. Auden's poetry derived its power base from a coincidence between private obsessions and public circumstances. What began as individualistic disaffection, a counter-culture to the public-school ethos (although imprinted by it), widened to embrace the whole condition of England at a period when the Depression and the rise of European Fascism were putting the national health to the test. The first poem in *New Signatures* is an ode from *The Orators* in which Auden ironically mimics the fears of an Establishment discredited by the First World War, but still brainwashing youth to resist 'them', i.e. the threat of radical change:

They speak of things done on the frontier we were
never told,
The hidden path to their squat Pictish tower
They will never reveal, though kept without sleep, for
their code is
'Death to the squealer.'

They are brave, yes, though our newspapers mention
their bravery
In inverted commas.

Auden's rich but ambiguous early landscape of frontiers and passes, crumbling regimes and brave saboteurs, was translated by some imitators into an explicitly revolutionary scenario. His modes of oratory, too, were converted into manifestos by poets like Cecil Day Lewis and Stephen Spender. Spender's *Forward from Liberalism* (1937) represents a zenith of belief in the writer's obligation to align himself with the Communist position.

It should be remembered that what George Orwell terms 'the Soviet myth' remained largely intact throughout the 1930s. For many British left-wingers, Russia beckoned as a Utopian alternative to the dangerous advance of Fascism – which they perceived very accurately indeed. Essentially writers and intellectuals participated in a minority protest-movement, whose adherents would later be dubbed 'premature anti-Fascists' by conservatives slow or reluctant to question Hitler's intentions. Spender recalls in *The Thirties and After* (1978):

> up till the time of Munich the great majority of people in England were unaware of the reality of terror. If a small but vociferous and talented minority of what were called the 'intellectuals' (this was the decade in which this term began to be widely used or abused) were almost hypnotically aware of the Nazi nightmare, the vast majority of people – and the government and members of the ruling class – seemed determined to ignore or deny it. One had the sense of belonging to a small group who could see terrible things which no one else saw. This was the period of Stanley Baldwin's premiership, the Royal Jubilee, the British Empire Exhibition.

Although Auden's 'Spain' is a classic articulation of anti-Fascist emotion, his poetry never committed itself unequivocally to Communism. The humorous excess of 'A Communist to Others' as compared with Day Lewis's earnest prose homily 'to a Young Revolutionary' ('Dear Jonathan, So you are thinking of joining the Communist Party'), both of which appeared in *New Country*, supports the view that Marxism provided Auden with personae and structures rather than wholesale ideology:

> Their splendid people, their wiseacres,
> Professors, agents, magic-makers,
> Their poets and apostles,
> Their bankers and their brokers too,
> And ironmasters shall turn blue
> Shall fade away like morning dew
> With club-room fossils.

No wonder that Day Lewis complains in *A Hope for Poetry*:

> The force of [Auden's] satire is, however, diminished . . . he does not seem to discriminate sufficiently between the really sick and the merely hypochondriac: the old satirists had to have a very definite criterion for measuring good and evil; the new one, to be thoroughly successful, must have equally definite standards of sickness and health. Auden is an adept at saying Bo to invalids and taking away their rugs; but one feels that he does not really care whether the invalid is a malingerer or just recovering from pneumonia. He is an expert at diagnosis, but has only one treatment for all ailments; we should feel happier if he evinced a love of health and a knowledge of its nature equivalent to his love and ability of diagnosis.

MacNeice never took Auden seriously as a messiah, although he took him very seriously as a poet. In *Modern Poetry* he emphasizes the artistic fruitfulness of Auden's approach, not its political usefulness: 'Auden . . . has the advantage of seeing the world both in terms of psycho-analysis and of a Marxian doctrine of progress. Thereby nearly all the detail in the world becomes significant for him' (p. 25). And while MacNeice applauds the *New Signatures* poets for being 'emotionally partisan', his preface to *Modern Poetry* does not compromise on the distinction between poetry and propaganda:

> Poetry today should steer a middle course between pure entertainment ('escape poetry') and propaganda. Propaganda, the extreme development of 'critical' poetry, is also the defeat of criticism. And the mere slogan-poet contradicts his name –

poietes, a 'maker'. The poet is a maker, not a retail trader. The writer today should be not so much the mouthpiece of a community (for then he will only tell it what it knows already) as its conscience, its critical faculty, its generous instinct. In a world intransigent and over-specialized, falsified by practical necessities, the poet must maintain his elasticity and refuse to tell lies to order. Others can tell lies more efficiently; no one except the poet can give us poetic truth.

Earlier (October 1934) a *New Verse* questionnaire had asked poets: 'Do you take your stand with any political or politico-economic party or creed?' MacNeice replied: 'No. In weaker moments I wish I could' (*SCLM*, p. 4).

Hynes finds MacNeice a fertile source of demythologizing comments on his contemporaries: proof that he functioned critically between attachment and detachment. It was MacNeice who coined the phrase 'myths of themselves' to denote the degree of literary posture in some political stances. *I Crossed the Minch* contains a flippant dialogue between MacNeice and his 'Guardian Angel' in which he dramatizes his reluctance to acquire an 'attitude':

G.A.: Well, what shall we talk about? Have you read that nice book by your friend Spender yet? Forward from something.

Me: *Forward from Liberalism.*

G.A.: That's it – *Forward from Liberalism.* I've always been a bit of a Liberal myself – pink as they say. And that reminds me – speaking in my professional capacity, don't you think it's almost time *you* had an attitude on these subjects?

Me: Why?

G.A.: Well, it seems to be the thing to do. Tell the world, you know.

Me: You think the world would be the least little teeny bit interested? Besides I can't tell the world what I think before I've thought it . . .

Me: My sympathies are Left. On paper and in the soul. But not in my heart or my guts. On paper – yes.

> I would vote Left any day, sign manifestos, answer questionnaires. Ditto, my soul. My soul is all for moving towards the classless society. But unlike Plato, what my soul says does not seem to go.
>
> (pp. 124–5)

In *The Strings are False*, wartime retrospect sharpens MacNeice's tone:

> The English Labour Party is notoriously lacking in glamour; these young poets had turned to the tomb of Lenin, the great flirtation had begun with the Third International. The strongest appeal of the Communist Party was that it demanded sacrifice; you had to sink your ego. At the moment there seemed to be a confusion between the state and the community, and I myself was repelled by the idolization of the state; but that was all right, it is written: 'The state shall wither away.' Young men were swallowing Marx with the same naïve enthusiasm that made Shelley swallow Rousseau.
>
> (pp. 145–6)

After Auden had become convinced, in the words of his elegy for Yeats, that 'poetry makes nothing happen', he similarly observed: 'I have never yet met a Left-wing intellectual for whom the real appeal of Communism did not lie in its romantic promise that with the triumph of Communism the State shall wither away' ('The Prolific and the Devourer', 1939).

MacNeice's longer-standing irony was influenced by his having witnessed the representative conversion of Anthony Blunt from aestheticism to Marxism. In early 1936 he visited Blunt at Cambridge, 'still full of Peter Pans but all the Peter Pans were now talking Marx' (*SAF*, p. 156). He was not only amused but, like Orwell, frightened by the surrender of intellectuals to totalitarian habits of mind, to strategic imperatives: 'After a bit the Marxist, who is only human, finds it such fun practising strategy – i.e. hypocrisy, lying, graft, political pimping, tergiversation, allegedly necessary murder – that he forgets the end in the means, the evil of the means drowns the good of the end, power corrupts, the living gospel withers, Siberia fills with ghosts' (*SAF*, p. 161). The collapse of the 1930s as matter for poetic myth-making, or rather transition to the myth's phase of disillusionment, is encapsulated in MacNeice's account of how orthodox Communists received Spender's play *Trial of a Judge*:

> And another thing – the Comrades went on – this play gives expression to feelings of anxiety, fear and depression; which is wrong because . . . S. said if they felt no anxiety themselves, well he felt sorry for them. Lastly, an old man got up, very sincere, very earnest, toilworn. There was one thing about the play, he said, which especially worried him; of course he knew S. could not have meant it, there must have been a mistake, but the writing seemed to imply an acceptance of Abstract Justice, a thing which we know is non-existent. S. deliberately towered into blasphemy. Abstract Justice, he said, of course he meant it; and what was more it existed.
>
> After that S. gradually fell away from the Party; he had not been born for dogma. (*SAF*, p. 168)

In *The Thirties and After* Spender quotes the passage against himself.

Because MacNeice had never subscribed to the original myth, he underwent no volte-face (Day Lewis), anguished retreat backwards from Communism (Spender), or regrouping of aesthetic ideas (Auden). Significantly, it was Yeats who focused his disagreement with Auden at the end of the decade: 'It is an historical fact that art *can* make things happen and Auden in his reaction from a rigid Marxism seems in ['The Public v. the Late Mr William Butler Yeats'] to have been straying towards the Ivory Tower' (*PWBY*, p. 192). MacNeice's own views evolved, but not by pendulum-swings – and never in the direction of ivory towers. His mid-1930s essay 'Poetry Today', while declaring 'I have no patience with those who think that poetry for the rest of the history of mankind will be merely a handmaid of Communism', considers 'intoxication with a creed . . . a good antidote to defeatist individualism' (*SCLM*, p. 25). It is true that, unlike *A Hope for Poetry*, *Modern Poetry* does not dwell on poetry's relevance to 'the society some of us hope for and are fighting for'. MacNeice concentrates on what 'A Change of Attitude' means *for poetry itself*. Nevertheless, the new aesthetic promoted by the book also amounts to a step forward from old-style literary liberalism. The 'Change of Attitude' chapter ends:

> The poet is once again to make his response as a whole. On the one side is concrete living – not just a conglomeration of animals or machines, mere flux, a dissolving hail of data, but a system of individuals determined by their circumstances, a concrete, therefore, of sensuous fact and what we may call 'universals'; on the other side is a concrete poet – not just an eye or a heart or a brain or a solar plexus, but the whole man reacting with both intelligence and emotion (which is how we react to anything in ordinary life) to experiences . . .
> (pp. 29–30)

Perhaps no Irish writer – and the above moves forward from Yeats's unities of being and culture – is ever a liberal in quite the English sense. The essayist Hubert Butler (in *Escape from the Anthill*, 1985) brings an Anglo-Irish perspective to bear on autobiographies by two of MacNeice's thirties contemporaries:

> [Graham] Greene is buttoned up securely into his close-fitting philosophy, while [Stephen] Spender is always unbuttoning his looser one. Yet I would say that their obsession with buttons brings them curiously near to each other and makes them fit representatives of their age. They are both constantly concerned with life and society and the restraints that men should and should not impose on each other.

MacNeice's shaping antinomies produced different results from the English 'obsession with buttons'. Auden and others were struggling within a hierarchical and long-established society, which 'Woods' perceives as 'An ordered open air long ruled by dyke and fence'. Coming from the 'wilds' of a more primitively politicized culture, MacNeice understood where literature ends and real politics begins. He stands on the other side of this boundary from a younger poet, John Cornford. Also amused by 'the intelligentsia playing at revolution', Cornford decided that full-time commitment to Communism must relegate the writing of poetry to the sidelines. MacNeice met him during the visit to Cambridge and described him as 'the first inspiring communist I had met'. Cornford actively went forward from the liberalism of his Bloomsbury parents. MacNeice, with Yeats as an example, showed more stamina than most in holding to poetry itself as a form of action. Stamina characterizes his reply (1941) to 'The Leaning Tower', Virginia Woolf's attack on the thirties writers:

> Recantation is becoming too fashionable; I am sorry to see so much self-flagellation, so many *Peccavis*, going on on the literary Left. We may not have done all we could in the Thirties, but we did do something. We were right to throw mud at Mrs Woolf's old horses and we were right to advocate social reconstruction and we were even right – in our more lyrical work – to give personal expression to our feelings of anxiety, horror and despair (for even despair can be fertile). As for the Leaning Tower, if Galileo had not had one at Pisa, he would not have discovered the truth about falling weights. We learned something of the sort from our tower too. (*SCLM*, pp. 123–4)

2

The oddly-worded blurb of MacNeice's *Poems* (1935) calls him 'intensely serious without political enthusiasm'. Certainly three poems, 'To a Communist', 'The Individualist Speaks' and 'Turf-Stacks', arrive on the thirties scene as a rebuke to revolutionary intelligentsia. 'To a Communist', reversing familiar personae of Auden, Spender and Day Lewis, preaches against the converted:

> Your thoughts make shape like snow; in one night only
> The gawky earth grows breasts,
> Snow's unity engrosses
> Particular pettiness of stones and grasses.
> But before you proclaim the millennium, my dear,
> Consult the barometer –
> This poise is perfect but maintained
> For one day only.

In 'Turf-Stacks' western landscape and its inhabitants rouse MacNeice's distaste for their opposite: the 'mass-production of neat thoughts' and the

Shuddering insidious shock of the theory-vendors,
The little sardine men crammed in a monster toy
Who tilt their aggregate beast against our crumbling Troy.

Later, Hebridean communal life was to stiffen this line of resistance: 'A world society must be a federation of differentiated communities, not a long line of robots doing the goose-step' (*ICTM*, p. 12). 'The Individualist Speaks' – a daring persona – begins by portraying bourgeois society as a tawdry fairground, in a way that both admits and satirizes the Marxist charge:

We with our Fair pitched among the feathery clover
Are always cowardly and never sober,
Drunk with steam-organs, thigh-rub and cream soda
– We cannot remember enemies in this valley.

The last line evokes Auden's landscape, as does the prospect of 'Avenging youth threatening an old war'. However, the individualist ultimately distances himself from the undeviating, if salutary, momentum of revolution:

Crawling down like lava or termites
Nothing seduces, nothing dissolves, nothing affrights
You who scale off masks and smash the purple lights
– But I will escape, with my dog, on the far side of the Fair.

'My dog' is an inconsequent touch which validates the projected 'escape' as more non-conformism than ivory-towerism. Yet the poem may pose, rather than judge between, the alternatives of Communism and the individualist 'atom thinking about himself'.

Certainly the hothouse solipsism in *Blind Fireworks* has disappeared from *Poems*. Or rather, it cools into one side of an emerging dialectic about responsibilities. MacNeice's own change of aesthetic attitude is at once a matter of creative maturation and a product of the wider context within which that maturation took place. Several poems broadly accept the Marxist critique of capitalism – crumbling Troy, doomed Fair – while stopping short of revolutionary hopes. Indeed, 'An Eclogue for Christmas' starts off the collection by directly addressing 'an evil time'. The 'Eclogue' reflects, and reflects on (see page 98), transition from the literary 1920s to the literary 1930s. Mac-

Neice's version of the Decline of the West owes something to *The Waste Land* as well as to *Das Kapital*: a hybridization common in works of the period. Like Eliot, he heaps up images of a civilization which has lost its way:

A. The tin toys of the hawker move on the pavement inch by inch
Not knowing that they are wound up; it is better to be so
Than to be, like us, wound up and while running down to know –
B. But everywhere the pretence of individuality recurs –
A. Old faces frosted with powder and choked in furs.
B. The jutlipped farmer gazing over the humpbacked wall.
A. The commercial traveller joking in the urinal.
B. I think things draw to an end, the soil is stale.

However, in replacing Eliot's elusive voices with official spokesmen for town and country, MacNeice breaks with the mode of *The Waste Land*. The 'Eclogue' also documents and comments in a manner alien to what C. K. Stead terms Eliot's 'pure, non-discursive Image' (*The New Poetic*). Again, its vision approximates more closely to Auden's metaphors for a neurotic society than to Eliot's symbolic spiritual desert. 'A' diagnoses 'The excess sugar of a diabetic culture / Rotting the nerve of life and literature'. Here 'culture', 'nerve', 'life and literature' carry social meanings with which *The Waste Land* is not primarily concerned. The people in the 'Eclogue' are socially symptomatic, and MacNeice ascribes some of their moral emptiness to dependence on a corrupt class system: 'The flotsam of private property . . . The good things which in the end turn to poison and pus'. And if, apart from prophesying an 'end', the poem omits the politics of a Spender or Day Lewis, it also omits Eliot's implicit theology. MacNeice remains humanistically absorbed by everyday life. He pronounces in *Modern Poetry*: 'the contemplation of a world of fragments becomes boring and Eliot's successors are more interested in tidying it up' (p. 13). The dialectic of 'An Eclogue for Christmas', veers between 1920s fatalism ('I turn this jaded music on / To forswear thought and become an automaton') and the dawn of 1930s resolve (to reiterate 'The old idealist lie').

The overall trajectory parallels the revelation MacNeice credits to his experience of Birmingham:

> living in a large industrial city, Birmingham, I recognized that the squalor of Eliot was a romanticized squalor because treated, on the whole, rather bookishly as *décor*. The 'short square fingers stuffing pipes' were not brute romantic objects abstracted into a picture by Picasso, but were living fingers attached to concrete people – were even, in a sense, *my* fingers. (*MP*, p. 74)

Even read as a mere change of literary pose, that recognition marks a boundary between decades.

While neither speaker in the 'Eclogue' expects much from a 'new régime' installed by 'the sniggering machine-guns in the hands of the young men', the 'ephemeral things' that modify this chorus of doom amount to more than fragments shored against ruins:

> A. But yet there is beauty narcotic and deciduous
> In this vast organism grown out of us:
> On all the traffic-islands stand white globes like moons,
> The city's haze is clouded amber that purrs and croons,
> And tilting by the noble curve bus after tall bus comes
> With an osculation of yellow light, with a glory like chrysanthemums.

MacNeice has not yet received his due for making urban landscapes part of the regular fabric of poetry. Derek Mahon suggests: 'If Dublin could be reconstructed from the pages of *Ulysses*, as Joyce claimed, the pre-war urban England of rainy tramlines, Corner Houses, Bisto Kids and Guinness Is Good For You could probably be roughly simulated from a reading of Greene and MacNeice' (*Time Was Away*, ed. Brown and Reid). Like 'Birmingham', written a few months earlier, 'An Eclogue for Christmas' heralds one of MacNeice's special contributions to the tidying up of fragments, or a socially alert aesthetic: his belief that the poet should include the journalist. Auden shared this belief; but his journalism tends towards editorial and comment, whereas MacNeice's largely belongs to the features pages. In 'Poetry Today'

MacNeice observes that 'Auden, the journalist, runs the danger of merely showing off [his opinions], of pamphleteering' (*SCLM*, p. 37). (His own danger is excess data.) The main characteristics of MacNeice's poetic journalism are: sensory receptivity, catalogues of society's 'variousness', condensed sociology. His cityscapes, then, epitomize his effort as a 'concrete poet' to render 'concrete living'. He puts flesh on the social world of 1930s poetry, a world whose concreteness was threatened by romantic abstraction of a different type to Eliot's.

Yet MacNeice's early urban impressions occupy an intermediate zone between Eliot's 'décor' and Philip Larkin's (almost) matter-of-fact. The passage quoted above from the 'Eclogue' makes the city Romantically seductive ('beauty narcotic and deciduous'), the stuff of Impressionist paintings; and it emphasizes beauty by extending the values of the natural world, of 'Mayfly', to an inorganic 'organism': 'osculation of yellow light . . . a glory like chrysanthemums'. Similarly, even the hostile 'Belfast' reprieves industrialism from dullness by serving it up as Gothic horror. 'Birmingham' too, although again a poem of protest, stops at nothing to heighten an unglamorous subject:

Smoke from the train-gulf hid by hoardings blunders upward, the brakes of cars
Pipe as the policeman pivoting round raises his flat hand, bars
With his figure of a monolith Pharaoh the queue of fidgety machines
(Chromium dogs on the bonnet, faces behind the triplex screens).
Behind him the streets run away between the proud glass of shops,
Cubical scent-bottles artificial legs arctic foxes and electric mops,
But beyond this centre the slumward vista thins like a diagram:
There, unvisited, are Vulcan's forges who doesn't care a tinker's damn.

It is hardly 'journalism' to term a traffic-policeman 'a monolith Pharaoh', or factories 'Vulcan's forges', or (as in the 'Eclogue') to perceive city lights and colours with hallucinatory intensity: 'Pentecost-like . . . crème-de-menthe or bull's blood'. This pictorial and metaphorical kaleidoscope is no 'dissolving hail'. Nor does it freeze into either Cubist or Marxist abstraction. MacNeice builds up a single felt image of Birmingham.

However, what coheres in the poem is regarded by the poem as itself 'incoherent', a disjunction between human beings and their environment. In using the simile of Pre-Raphaelite windows 'broken' by metal, MacNeice draws on a tradition of opposition between art and industrialism, even while implying his own ability to portray an industrialized and commercialized society:

The lunch hour: the shops empty, shopgirls' faces relax
Diaphanous as green glass, empty as old almanacs
As incoherent with ticketed gewgaws tiered behind their heads
As the Burne-Jones windows in St Philip's broken by crawling
leads . . .

Above all, MacNeice's urban landscapes are peopled landscapes. As social criticism, Birmingham indicts the exploitation of factory workers and shop-girls, exploitation connived at by the upwardly mobile who 'endeavour to find God and score one over the neighbour / By climbing tentatively upward on jerry-built beauty and sweated labour.' But the irony indicates that D. H. Lawrence has influenced the poem as much as Karl Marx. MacNeice not only accuses capitalism of breeding injustice, he accuses materialism of short-changing the spirit. Nature and tradition are denied by houses with 'only a six-inch grip of the racing earth in their concrete claws'; imagination and love by 'Insipid colour, patches of emotion, Saturday thrills' (all antithetical to what the poem itself has to offer). By a process of alarming exchange, here the inorganic eats into the organic or assumes an oppressive life of its own: screened faces, 'the heart's funfair', 'fidgety machines', 'proud glass', 'concrete claws'. The favourite words 'gewgaws' and 'gadgets' sum up the artificial appetites promoted by commerce. In one sense MacNeice's powers of observation and absorption relish what he condemns. But this is the inherent paradox of poetic subject matter rather than any suspect attraction to surfaces. Two later poems, 'Christmas Shopping' and 'Bagpipe Music', continue his critique of consumerism.

'Christmas Shopping' tracks 'the sewers of money' to the image of a *deus ex machina*:

> Further out on the coast the lighthouse moves its
> Arms of light through the fog that wads our welfare,
> Moves its arms like a giant at Swedish drill whose
> Mind is a vacuum.

That is one way of highlighting the huge, indifferent forces at work in the economic system. In 'Bagpipe Music' MacNeice employs satirical rhythms to underline the dissonance between contemporary forms of greed and traditional culture, as exemplified by his Hebridean Utopia:

> Willie Murray cut his thumb, couldn't count the damage,
> Took the hide of an Ayrshire cow and used it for a bandage.
> His brother caught three hundred cran when the seas were lavish,
> Threw the bleeders back in the sea and went upon the parish.
>
> It's no go the Herring Board, it's no go the Bible,
> All we want is a packet of fags when our hands are idle.

Published in *The Earth Compels* (1938), these poems may react to economic and political sickness beyond the coasts of Britain. But the unifying symbolism of 'Birmingham' already seems sinister enough. A deathly tyranny over the lives of individuals, the social face of petrifaction, is communicated by 'Pharaoh . . . Vulcan . . . concrete claws . . . crawling leads . . . trams like vast sarcophagi . . . the factory chimneys on sullen sentry'.

Letters from Iceland appeared between *Poems* and *The Earth Compels*. MacNeice says: 'Our travel-book was a hodge-podge, thrown together in gaiety' (*SAF*, p. 164); but this is half-disingenuous. Iceland gave him and Auden a new vantage point from which to reflect on literature and society. Like 'Bagpipe Music', *Letters* acts on a further shared belief of the two poets: that poetry should be a kind of fun as well as a kind of journalism. (Humour is conspicuously absent from the work of Spender and Day Lewis.) Not only is the poet ideally 'both critic and entertainer', but 'his criticism will cut no ice unless he entertains' (*MP*, Preface). Auden's 'Letter to Lord Byron', the book's finest achievement, expresses as well as fulfils that aesthetic. Auden celebrates Byron as 'the master of the airy manner' and defends the comic Muse:

> By all means let us touch our humble caps to
> La poésie pure, the epic narrative;
> But comedy shall get its round of claps, too.
> According to his powers, each may give;
> Only on varied diet can we live.
> The pious fable and the dirty story
> Share in the total literary glory.

MacNeice's chapter in *Modern Poetry* on 'Lighter Poetry and Drama' (which celebrates Auden) defines the 'two poles of lighter poetry' as 'the "Grain of Salt" and the "Urge to Nonsense" ' (p. 179) – a variant of criticism and entertainment. In *Letters* the pure Urge to Nonsense produces some of the notes 'For Tourists' ('There is not much to be said for Reykjavik'), a collage of wickedly chosen comments from other travellers, and 'Hetty to Nancy'. The latter is a prose spoof-epistle from MacNeice to Anthony Blunt in the persona of one young woman writing to another about her trip with a girlfriend: 'To see Maisie struggling out of her undies in two square foot of space makes you realize what built the British Empire.' MacNeice demythologizes again. The nonsense and gaiety in *Letters* have the air of enjoyable truancy from the political and literary- political pressures of the 1930s. As MacNeice puts it in 'Postscript to Iceland' (originally 'Epilogue'):

> Holidays should be like this,
> Free from over-emphasis,
> Time for soul to stretch and spit
> Before the world comes back on it . . .

Similarly, the aesthetic of 'Letter to Lord Byron' is partly one of liberation. Nevertheless, the world and the European news 'came back on' the poets, if they had ever truly receded:

> Down in Europe Seville fell,
> Nations germinating hell,
> The Olympic games were run –

Spots upon the Aryan sun.
('Postscript')

Auden says in his Foreword to the 1967 reprint of *Letters*:

> Though writing in a 'holiday' spirit, its authors were all the time conscious of a threatening horizon to their picnic – world-wide unemployment, Hitler growing every day more powerful and a world-war more inevitable. Indeed, the prologue to that war, the Spanish Civil War, broke out while we were there.

Apart from 'Hetty to Nancy', MacNeice's main contributions to *Letters* were: 'Letter to Graham and Anna' (originally 'Letter to Graham and Anne Shepard'), 'Eclogue from Iceland', 'Postscript', and his collaboration in 'Last Will and Testament'. 'Letter to Graham and Anna' fails to match 'Letter to Lord Byron' as a blend of the 'airy' and substantial:

But what am I doing here? Qu'allais-je faire
Among these volcanic rocks and this grey air?
Why go north when Cyprus and Madeira
De jure if not de facto are much nearer?
The reason for hereness seems beyond conjecture,
There are no trees or trains or architecture . . .

MacNeice lacks Auden's light hand with Byronic rhyme, and he can be ponderous when modulating into seriousness: 'We are not changing ground to escape from facts / But rather to find them.' The best passages once again affirm 'The necessity of the silence of the islands' as an antidote to noise and rush; but a later poem 'Iceland' puts this more stringently:

The glacier's licking
Tongues deride
Our pride of life,
Our flashy songs.

MacNeice makes a better job of the light verse-epistle or flashy song in 'Last Will and Testament', which belongs solely to *Letters* and not to either poet's *Collected Poems*. This is the book's quintessential 'hodge-podge': a rag-bag of in-jokes and topical lampoons at the expense of friends, family, England, Ireland, church and state, artistic and intellectual life, well-known public figures. The poets seem to name everyone they can think of. Although a period piece which does not pretend otherwise, 'Last Will and Testament' looks beyond the period on behalf of the seriously held values which inform its gaiety. The poem is thus also quintessential in its tone, a tone which merges the voices of Auden and MacNeice. Its strengths and limitations, like those of *Letters from Iceland* as a whole, might be used to test the success of 'thirties poetry' as a corporate enterprise. Hynes comments: 'the poets distribute the things of their own familiar world among their friends and enemies, as though they were writing not *their* will but the *world's*, drawn up in expectation of its imminent death' (*TAG*, p. 290). Thus MacNeice places personal bequests in a context of provision for general survival:

> L. And I to all my friends would leave a ration
> Of bread and wit against the days which slant
> Upon us black with nihilistic passion.
>
> Item I leave my old friend Anthony Blunt
> A copy of Marx and £1000 a year
> And the picture of Love Locked Out by Holman Hunt.

The poem's public satire, while good-humoured, does not spare politicians, the 'purulent name' of Sir Oswald Mosley, England's need of 'an honest foreign policy'. Yet the testament confirms a shift for Auden if not for MacNeice, in being more essentially moral than political. The poets' final call to 'action' contrasts with the revolutionary war cries of the early 1930s:

> And to the good who know how wide the gulf, how deep
> Between Ideal and Real, who being good have felt
> The final temptation to withdraw, sit down and weep,
>
> We pray the power to take upon themselves the guilt
> Of human action, though still as ready to confess
> The imperfection of what can and must be built,
> The wish and power to act, forgive, and bless.

'Postscript' ends *Letters from Iceland* with waiting rather than activity:

Our prerogatives as men
Will be cancelled who knows when;
Still I drink your health before
The gun-butt raps upon the door.

This poem is MacNeice's most integrated use of Iceland as an imaginative focus, perhaps because retrospect has clarified the tension defined in 'a fancy turn, you know, / Sandwiched in a graver show'. Like 'The Closing Album', 'Postscript' layers past and present, pastoral and premonition:

Rows of books around me stand,
Fence me round on either hand;
Through that forest of dead words
I would hunt the living birds –

Great black birds that fly alone
Slowly through a land of stone,
And the gulls who weave a free
Quilt of rhythm on the sea.

But a postscript or epilogue, by definition, enters a new phase: in this case both historical and aesthetic. In fact the poem acts as a prologue to *Autumn Journal* since it projects a solitary consciousness who inhabits a world without the residual communal shelter of 'Last Will and Testament': 'All the wires are cut, my friends / Live beyond the severed ends.' 'Eclogue from Iceland' derives more immediately from 'our Iceland trip' and from the concerns of the mid-1930s. The special position of island holidays in MacNeice's mythology helps to create an allegorical forum for the relentless thirties debate about 'commitments'.

MacNeice divides the dialectic of 'Eclogue from Iceland' between Craven and Ryan (thin masks for Auden and MacNeice), the ghost of the Icelandic saga hero Grettir, and 'Voice from Europe'. The two latter contend for the souls of the two former. Speaking partly as poets, Craven and Ryan stand self-accused of evasion and irresponsibility:

R. And so we came to Iceland –
C. Our latest joyride.
G. And what have you found in Iceland?

C. What have we found? More copy, more surface,
   Vignettes as they call them, dead flowers in an album –

They also accuse their own societies: Ireland 'built upon violence' and akin to the vengeful ethos of saga; the 'dyspeptic age of ingrown cynics' to which Auden has been psychotherapist; the particularly cynical inequalities of England where the war hero 'With his ribbons and his empty pinned-up sleeve / Cadges for money'. The Voice from Europe, echoing the 'jaded music' in 'An Eclogue for Christmas', is the voice of post-war hedonism, of moral inertia: 'Who cares / If floods depopulate China?'

Grettir, 'doomed tough' rather than decadent softy, articulates the opposite attitude. Like the legendary Cuchulain in Yeats's interior drama, he functions as an archetype of action, unquestioning commitment, and full-blooded instinct. Doom embraces and braces him.

I wore it gracefully,
The fatal clarity that would not budge
But without false pride in martyrdom. For I,
Joker and dressy, held no mystic's pose,
Not wishing to die preferred the daily goods
The horse-fight, women's thighs, a joint of meat.

This is both an artistic and moral role model, scaled down from Yeatsian heights (neither martyr nor superman). MacNeice also imitates Yeats's methods in that he interleaves Grettir's autobiography with mythologized versions of other culture heroes, men of art and of action who kept faith under pressure:

C. There was that dancer
   Who danced the War, then falling into coma
   Went with hunched shoulders through the ivory gate.
R. There was Connolly
   Vilified now by the gangs of Catholic Action.

Given the last word in the argument, Grettir commits Ryan and Craven to personal and literary obligations: 'Go back to where you belong . . . every country stands / By the sanctity of the individual will.' Here MacNeice's non-defeatist individualism takes on collective urgency as an ethic of resistance to the totalitarian 'wall / Of shouting flesh'. If 'Eclogue from Iceland' is the most political of his eclogues it is because humanist values, 'Our prerogatives as men', are now on the political agenda:

> G. Minute your gesture but it must be made –
> Your hazard, your act of defiance and hymn of hate,
> Hatred of hatred, assertion of human values,
> Which is now your only duty.
> C. Is it our only duty?
> G.   Yes, my friends.
> What did you say? The night falls now and I
> Must beat the dales to chase my remembered acts.
> Yes, my friends, it is your only duty.
> And, it may be added, it is your only chance.

And in so far as this is an agenda for poetry too, *Autumn Journal* will carry it out.

III
Autumn Journal

All the currents of MacNeice's writing during the 1930s flow into *Autumn Journal* and find a new dynamic there: lyrics, eclogues, prose, the Audenesque play *Out of the Picture*, images, strategies, tones of voice. His entire creative kaleidoscope breaks up and re-forms. A note from MacNeice to T. S. Eliot at Faber indicates both the scope he had in mind, and the extent to which the 'tenor' of five months took over his imagination:

> *Autumn Journal*:
>
> A long poem from 2,000 to 3,000 lines written from August to December 1938. Not strictly a journal but giving the tenor of my intellectual and emotional experiences during that period.
>
> It is about nearly everything which from firsthand experience I consider significant.
>
> It is written in sections averaging about 80 lines in length. This division gives it a *dramatic* quality, as different parts of myself (e.g. the anarchist, the defeatist, the sensual man, the philosopher, the would-be good citizen) can be given their say in turn.
>
> It contains rapportage, metaphysics, ethics, lyrical emotion, autobiography, nightmare . . . (quoted by Robyn Marsack in *The Cave of Making*)

At the simplest level, some familiar images reappear in freshly significant contexts. For instance, the morbid 'River in Spate' becomes an omen of the future as coloured by 'panic and self-deception': 'all we foresee is rivers in spate sprouting / With drowning hands' (VII). Conversely, MacNeice's positive image of moving water celebrates the motivating energy imparted by a loved woman who transforms life into 'a ladder of angels, river turning tidal' (IV). As for larger-scale realignments: I have already noted the greater precision of MacNeice's Irish valedictions and maledictions, as well as their new relevance to British and European politics. Similarly, section IV is a love poem with a difference, although addressed to the same 'alive' lady as 'Leaving Barra'. When her 'vitality leaps in the autumn', it now partly instances the protagonist's renewed social faith that 'there will always be people / For friends or for lovers'. On the darker side, section XV employs MacNeice's mode of nightmare to convey the horror and guilt that haunts Europe. A file of apparitions 'Following the track from the gallows back to the town' connects 'black dreams' with historical slaughters and betrayals:

> But something about their faces is familiar;
>   Where have we seen them before?
> Was it the murderer on the nursery ceiling
>   Or Judas Iscariot in the Field of Blood
> Or someone at Gallipoli or in Flanders
>   Caught in the end-all mud?

These rhetorical questions also connect personal, public and spiritual points of reference. Such unification of MacNeice's subjects and systems is fundamental to the poem. Thus at the end of section XX the theme of 'Christmas Shopping' acquires further dimensions which include nostalgia for 'childhood's thrill', and a revolutionary Christ 'knocking the heads / Of Church and State together'. Finally the Christmas story becomes a contemporary accusation:

> And Conscience still goes crying through the desert
>   With sackcloth round his loins:
> A week to Christmas – hark the herald angels
>   Beg for copper coins.

Autumn Journal is an act of imaginative conscience in desert times. MacNeice's note to Eliot defines the poem as 'both a panorama and a confession of faith'. The passages already cited show that it simultaneously represents the condition of a society in crisis, and formulates an emotional, social, political and 'ethical' response to that crisis. In early Autumn 1938 people went to their 'daily / Jobs to the dull refrain of the caption "War" ' (V).

Amid 'Conferences, adjournments, ultimatums' (VII) Neville Chamberlain pursued his policy of appeasing Hitler. The Munich agreement of late September, which sacrificed Czechoslovakia for the sake of an illusory 'peace for our time', is at the centre of *Autumn Journal* and centrally on its conscience. MacNeice places this shameful anti-climax at the climax of section VIII:

> But once again
>   The crisis is put off and things look better
> And we feel negotiation is not vain –
>   Save my skin and damn my conscience.
> And negotiation wins,
>   If you can call it winning,
> And here we are – just as before – safe in our skins;
>   Glory to God for Munich.
> And stocks go up and wrecks
>   Are salved and politicians' reputations
> Go up like Jack-on-the-Beanstalk; only the Czechs
>   Go down and without fighting.

But the causes of Munich lay far back. *Autumn Journal* examines the collective conscience by viewing the present in the light of the past and the past in the light of the present: 'Time is a country, the present moment / A spotlight roving round the scene' (XXIV). MacNeice's spotlight roves over the previous decade, British history after the First World War, even the history of western culture. The thirties poets had spoken of an end since the beginning, a trope satirized by William Empson in 'Just a Smack at Auden': 'Waiting for the end boys, waiting for the end'. However, the actual end in sight did not follow either left-wing or right-wing scripts. Hence perhaps the need to go back to the start of the story or myth and reread it – which MacNeice, more than any other writer, did.

MacNeice's poems from late 1936 to 1938 had already been saturated with valediction and dark anticipation: 'Last Will and Testament', 'Postscript to Iceland', elegiac lyrics in *Out of the Picture* which ends with an air raid on London, the 'empty dining hall' of 'The Brandy Glass', the elemental symbols of 'June Thunder' and 'The Sunlight on the Garden'. The latter, with its apt quotation from *Antony and Cleopatra* – 'We are dying, Egypt, dying' – powerfully realizes the threat to the world of personal emotion from the world of war: 'Our freedom as free lances / Advances towards its end'. But *Autumn Journal* is not just the ending poem to end all ending poems. Nor does it simply confirm the end of waiting. It synthesizes the loose ends of the 1930s into a personal and communal psychodrama which, as opposed to unhealthy suppressions, may have the effect of salvaging some prospects for the future from the wreck of the past. The process begins with a comprehensive ending and some initial perspectives on how it has come about:

Close and slow, summer is ending in Hampshire,
  Ebbing away down ramps of shaven lawn where close-clipped
    yew
Insulates the lives of retired generals and admirals
  And the spyglasses hung in the hall and the prayer-books ready
    in the pew
And August going out to the tin trumpets of nasturtiums
  And the sunflowers' Salvation Army blare of brass
And the spinster sitting in a deck-chair picking up stitches
  Not raising her eyes to the noise of the 'planes that pass
Northward from Lee-on-Solent. Macrocarpa and cypress
  And roses on a rustic trellis and mulberry trees
And bacon and eggs in a silver dish for breakfast
  And all the inherited assets of bodily ease
And all the inherited worries, rheumatism and taxes,
  And whether Stella will marry and what to do with Dick
And the branch of the family that lost their money in Hatry
  And the passing of the *Morning Post* and of life's climacteric
And the growth of vulgarity, cars that pass the gate-lodge
  And crowds undressing on the beach . . .

The seasonal symbolism inaugurated here encompasses transition on many fronts. Section I telescopes the whole course of *Autumn Journal* by moving forward geographically, historically and sociologically, and by evoking the summer that ended in August 1914. The 'retired generals and admirals' must be implicated in 'the end-all mud', as they are in the bourgeois, conservative order they have reinforced since 1918. Their milieu is perceived not only as one of petrifaction ('all is old as flint or chalk or pine-needles'), but more gravely as a condition of 'insulation' against the reality of change: the planes, 'the growth of vulgarity'. Meanwhile, 'the rebels and the young / Have taken the train to town'. Such a contrast locates the last decade within the longer perspective; as does that between the protagonist ('in the train too now') and a more modish type of insulation than the knitting spinster:

> Surbiton, and a woman gets in, painted
> With dyed hair but a ladder in her stocking and eyes
> Patient beneath the calculated lashes,
> Inured for ever to surprise . . .

This portrait, like the mock thirties love song which follows, seems bitterly tinged by another ending – the poet's divorce. But, in a more complex manner than the Voice from Europe, it essentially seals a developing antithesis between dying social orders and conventions, and the true

> dying that brings forth
> The harder life, revealing the trees' girders,
> The frost that kills the germs of *laissez-faire* . . .

Based on actuality, this is a subtler version of the future scenarios in early thirties poetry. The protagonist's journey to London denotes acceptance of the momentum of history. Yet the poem's own dynamism is also centripetal and centrifugal:

> And so to London and down the ever-moving
> Stairs
> Where a warm wind blows the bodies of men together
> And blows apart their complexes and cares.

This prepares for Section II: the soliloquy of a solitary 'afraid in the web of night'. It establishes a pattern of mediation between a cast of thousands (admirals, generals, 'hiking cockney lovers', 'the rebels and the young', multiple 'complexes and cares'), and the individual consciousness. Such a pattern accords remarkably with Geoffrey Grigson's prescriptions for the poet the time needed: 'The only justified retreat is the loneliness from which everything and everybody is more visible, the loneliness in the centre and not on the edge'; 'What we need now is not the fanatic, but the critical moralist; and the one loneliness which is justified is Rilke's loneliness *surrounded by everything* thorough, exact, without slovenliness, impressionable, and honest' (*New Verse*, Autumn 1938).

However, not every commentator has found *Autumn Journal* psychologically or politically adequate to its task. Contemporary reaction included Julian Symons's labelling the poem 'The Bourgeois's Progress', and John Lehmann's condescension to it as 'rambling, facile, prosy at times, never very deep or certain in thought, rather too conspicuously elaborating the picture of an easy-going but attractive personality' (quoted by Robyn Marsack). These are attacks from the Left. Hynes, while fully appreciating the poem as 'a poignant last example of that insistent 'thirties theme, the interpenetration of public and private worlds' (*TAG*, p. 368), again in my view undervalues the complexity of its attitudes and persona. Earlier he describes MacNeice's 'self-proclaimed role of common man' as 'a kind of substitute for political commitment' and characterizes his sensibility as that of 'the professional lachrymose Irishman' given to 'habitual sentimental melancholy'. I have argued in chapter I that MacNeice's Irishness comes from a tougher stable than such a stereotype. Indeed, what he considered 'sentimental' was the politics of his English friends. Nor does his persona stick in a single 'melancholy' groove. It is by putting 'different parts of myself' on stage, by virtue of its '*dramatic* quality', that *Autumn Journal* transcends the limitation of the eclogues: i.e. 'the mere deliberating what to do / When neither the pros nor cons affect the pulses' (IV).

The prefatory Note announces: 'this poem is something half-way between the lyric and the didactic poem'. As 'Snow' indicates, between-states mean much in MacNeice. Whereas Auden's natural didacticism and discursiveness relish a portmanteau medium like the verse-epistle, MacNeice's natural lyricism required a lonely centre from which to launch didactic and other excursions. Thus 'rapportage, metaphysics, ethics' pivot on 'lyrical emotion, autobiography', the journal of record stems from the first-person diary. The poem's wholesale 'accountancy' – one of its self-referring metaphors – sets the balance sheet of autobiography alongside that of history. Just as the latter might interpret Munich, so the former might interpret divorce and the poet's current personal dilemmas. History and autobiography, of course, not only 'interpenetrate' but interpret one another. For example, a retrospect on married life in Birmingham precedes the immediate response to Munich:

> But Life was comfortable, life was fine
>   With two in a bed and patchwork cushions
> And checks and tassels on the washing-line,
>   A gramophone, a cat, and the smell of jasmine.
> The steaks were tender, the films were fun,
>   The walls were striped like a Russian ballet,
> There were lots of things undone
> . . .
> We slept in linen, we cooked with wine,
>   We paid in cash and took no notice
> Of how the train ran down the line
>   Into the sun against the signal.
> We lived in Birmingham through the slump –
>   Line your boots with a piece of paper –
> Sunlight dancing on the rubbish dump,
>   On the queues of men and the hungry chimneys.
> And the next election came –
>   Labour defeats in Erdington and Aston . . . (VIII)

The brilliantly chosen details suggest how individual practices, as well as general economic conditions, feed into political crisis. Also, this further instance of insulation against reality applies not only to domestic and public housekeeping but to marital relations. The collective 'mounting debit' now presents itself: 'No wife, no ivory tower, no funk-hole'. Such stripping-away of comforts and complacencies licenses the protagonist's function as 'common man' or Everyman, and contradicts Hynes's view of this as 'apolitical'. The prospect of war touches more layers of the poetic personality than does the 'retail trading' of opinions, as MacNeice later implied in the introductory chapter to *The Poetry of W. B. Yeats*: 'If the war made nonsense of Yeats's poetry and of all works that are called "escapist", it also made nonsense of the poetry that professes to be "realist" ' (pp. 17–18). *Autumn Journal* does not merely speak either for the melancholy poet bereft of ivory tower, or for the 'easy-going' uncommitted bloke. Indeed, the incompatibility of such readings suggests that the poem dramatizes our full human alarm when historical forces move fast:

> The cylinders are racing in the presses,
> The mines are laid,
> The ribbon plumbs the fallen fathoms of Wall Street,
> And you and I are afraid. (V)

However, the 'intercrossing / Coloured waters' of *Autumn Journal* are difficult to separate. Thus the quotations in the previous paragraph might as easily come under the heading of 'panorama', as under that of lyrical self-dramatization surrounded by society. The panoramas of *Autumn Journal* follow their prototypes in 'Birmingham' and 'An Eclogue for Christmas' in that they consist of accumulated close-ups rather than long-distance shots. Some further imperatives from Geoffrey Grigson are relevant:

> Fidelity to what we can see of objects is the beginning of sanity . . . it is fatal to treat the exterior world as a kind of handwriting, the only use of which is to make the interior world legible. The world of objects is our constant discipline. Desert it, and you become the mouth under the short moustache on the last night of Nuremberg. (*New Verse*, Autumn 1938)

For Grigson, close observation has become an aesthetic which carries moral and political implications. MacNeice puts the matter more casually in his note to Eliot: 'There is constant interrelation of abstract and concrete. Generalizations balanced by pictures . . .' That he has undergone the discipline of objects is proved by the literally 'journalistic' success of *Autumn Journal*, by the way in which it communicates an 'extraordinary visual and tactile sense of the period' (to quote Derek Mahon), of everydayness turning strange. Modifying the high colours of his earlier urban pictures, MacNeice charges the poem with the atmosphere of a changing London:

A smell of French bread in Charlotte Street, a rustle
  Of leaves in Regent's Park
And suddenly from the Zoo I hear a sea-lion
  Confidently bark. (V)

Hitler yells on the wireless,
  The night is damp and still
And I hear dull blows on wood outside my window;
  They are cutting down the trees on Primrose Hill.
The wood is white like the roast flesh of chicken,
  Each tree falling like a closing fan;
No more looking at the view from seats beneath the branches,
  Everything is going to plan;
They want the crest of this hill for anti-aircraft,
  The guns will take the view
And searchlights probe the heavens for bacilli
  With narrow wands of blue. (VII)

Panoramas embrace 'concrete' people, sensations and actions, as well as objects; and their sphere of operation is not confined to the present moment but covers phases in memory or history: the Ireland of childhood alongside that of today, schooldays, Birmingham of the early 1930s, Spain of Easter 1936, even the ancient world with which MacNeice's education has made him intimate:

The hair-splitters, the pedants, the hard-boiled sceptics
  And the Agora and the noise
Of the demagogues and the quacks; and the women pouring
  Libations over graves
And the trimmers at Delphi and the dummies at Sparta and lastly
  I think of the slaves . . . (IX)

'Pictures' and 'generalizations' – once again not absolutely watertight categories – blend in each panorama as they do in the panorama of the whole poem. The picture of 'Birmingham through the slump' is manifestly not just documentary: it typifies and analyses, and it moves towards symbol: 'Sunlight dancing on the rubbish dump'. Similarly, all the details of 'cutting down the trees on Primrose Hill' ramify into a centrally significant symbol. The simile of 'the roast flesh of chicken' helps to expose preparations for war as violating nature and normality. *Autumn Journal* infuses new menace into MacNeice's mechanistic imagery: 'The guns will take the view.' On the other hand, images like the smell of bread and the sea-lion's bark suggest that life, obstinately, goes on. As for the classical past, MacNeice later said in a sleeve-note to a recorded reading of section IX and other poems: 'far from being objective about the Ancient Greeks, I see them here in the light of the mood induced in me by Munich' (see below). Thus the discipline of objects, strategies of objectification, can serve finely diffused subjective aims.

MacNeice's habit of cataloguing comes into its own in the panoramas of *Autumn Journal*. Section I unfolds the crucial role of the conjunction 'and'. This obvious syntactical means of being 'surrounded by everything' is also a structural means of not forcing issues or pushing connections and generalizations; but rather of presenting things that coexist and letting patterns emerge. 'And you and I are afraid', for instance, does much more than simply add another detail. Section X is a panorama, dependent on 'and', which surveys MacNeice's time at Sherborne and Marlborough. It sets out from his current educational circumstances ('the M.A. gown, / Alphas and Betas, central heating, floor-polish') and goes on to list sense impressions ('Lifebuoy soap and muddy flannels'), emotions ('alarm and exhilaration'), the mental and physical life of schoolboys ('a heap of home-made dogma', 'the Fives-courts' tattling repartee' – which combines styles of talk with games). Yet this hail of data simultaneously contributes to an ironic movement whereby the school regime, with its bells and conformities, merges into the equally closed system of the society outside:

> But life began to narrow to what was done –
> The dominant gerundive –
> And Number Two must mimic Number One
> In bearing, swearing, attitude and accent.

Unlike 'the dominant gerundive' (the form of a Latin verb for stating what *must* be done) the syntax of *Autumn Journal* opens out. The entire poem, including the relation between sections, is an act of pluralistic conjunction, a series of links that evolve into a great chain.

MacNeice still approaches politics obliquely in *Autumn Journal*: otherwise he would not be using classical and Irish panoramas to relieve his post-Munich mood. These political worlds that he knows well enable him to develop the implications of 'Save my skin and damn my conscience' more profoundly than if he had merely railed at Chamberlain. The Greek world, less hypocritically than our own, exemplifies the roughness of power politics:

> And Alcibiades lived from hand to mouth
> Double-crossing Athens, Persia, Sparta,
> And many died in the city of plague, and many of drouth
> In Sicilian quarries, and many by the spear and arrow
> And many more who told their lies too late
> Caught in the eternal factions and reactions
> Of the city-state. (IX)

Later, 'the trimmers at Delphi and the dummies at Sparta' despises the makers of Munich, while 'and lastly / I think of the slaves' grimly sums up its consequences. But there are also more direct versions of contemporary politics in *Autumn Journal*, if less powerfully executed. Section III outlines a democratic Socialist Utopia:

> Where skill will no longer languish nor energy be trammelled
> To competition and graft,
> Exploited in subservience but not allegiance
> To an utterly lost and daft
> System that gives a few at fancy prices
> Their fancy lives . . .

At the same time MacNeice, like Orwell, honestly faces the difficulty of eliminating bourgeois reflexes, such as the 'highbrow's' prejudice 'that in order / To preserve the values dear to the élite / The élite must remain a few'. Thus while insisting: 'Which fears must be suppressed', this fallible Everyman personifies the problem of slotting real human beings, with their irrational selfishness and 'mixed motives', into ideal systems: 'If it were not for Lit.Hum. I might be climbing / A ladder with a hod' (XII).

The only political act on the part of the protagonist is his canvassing and voting in the Oxford by-election (XIV). This was one of several such elections in which an alliance between the Liberal and Labour parties, together with Conservative rebels, opposed pro-Munich Tories. The latter, in the person of the present Lord Hailsham, defeated A. D. Lindsay who stood as an Independent candidate. Oxford's 'coward vote' provokes a meditation on the goals and uses of democratic activity:

> And what am I doing it for?
> Mainly for fun, partly for a half-believed-in
> Principle, a core
> Of fact in a pulp of verbiage,
> Remembering that this crude and so-called obsolete
> Top-heavy tedious parliamentary system
> Is our only ready weapon to defeat
> The legions' eagles and the lictors' axes;
> And remembering that those who by their habit hate
> Politics can no longer keep their private
> Values unless they open the public gate
> To a better political system.

These conclusions are perhaps less significant for adhering to democracy as a defence against totalitarianism (symbolized by the neo-Roman insignia of Fascism) than for insisting that the current crisis *de facto* has politicized everyone.

Further, the phrase 'a core / Of fact in a pulp of verbiage', which might be a joke against the poem itself, suggests that *Autumn Journal* has found a political role for poetry in criticizing the effect of politics on language. The sections on the ancient world and Ireland (home of 'Purblind manifestoes') both refer to the silencing of dissent:

> And free speech shivered on the pikes of Macedonia
> And later on the swords of Rome . . . (IX)

> Free speech nipped in the bud,
> The minority always guilty. (XVI)

Elsewhere, politics produces 'blank invective', ideas 'travestied in slogans', 'A howling radio', 'The devil quoting scripture'. To back up its assault on propaganda, 'the defeat of criticism' according to *Modern Poetry*, the poem exposes contributory linguistic falsifications which promote false consciousness. Education, for instance, encourages 'too many labels / And clichés' (XII) i.e. insulated vocabularies that do not square with the facts of life now staring society in the face. MacNeice himself has acquired two 'dead' languages: the 'hall-marked marmoreal phrases' of Greek and Latin, and the autistic abstractions of philosophy as taught at Oxford:

> And they said 'The man in the street is so naïve, he never
> Can see the wood for the trees;
> He thinks he knows he sees a thing but cannot
> Tell you how he knows the thing he thinks he sees.'
> And oh how much I liked the Concrete Universal,
> I never thought that I should
> Be telling them vice-versa
> That they can't see the trees for the wood. (XIII)

This, like other passages, also indicts the limited *social* vocabulary of the privileged. Not only philosophical cliché but the rewriting of history serves to institutionalize myopia. Peter Parker in *The Old Lie* (1987) shows how the teaching of classics in the public schools before the First World War was distorted by heroic and patriotic myths. MacNeice nails a related lie:

> the humanist in his room with Jacobean panels
> Chewing his pipe and looking on a lazy quad
> Chops the Ancient World to turn a sermon
> To the greater glory of God.
> But I can do nothing so useful or so simple . . . (IX)

In fact MacNeice usefully reminds us that 'the paragons of Hellas' included 'The bloody Bacchanals on the Thracian hills'. The poem's own vocabulary makes a better job of both the ancient world and the Concrete Universal, since its catalogues put the trees back in the wood of ideology. In its attitudes to totalitarianism, and to the propagandist abuse of language and thought,

Autumn Journal anticipates Orwell's *Animal Farm* and *Nineteen Eighty-Four*.

Spain, the great testing-ground for the politically conscious writers of the 1930s, shaped those two fables of the 1940s. Orwell's 'Looking Back on the Spanish War' dissects the propaganda of the Republican government (uncritically swallowed by British left-wingers) and its still more monstrous Fascist counterpart (uncritically swallowed by British right-wingers): 'the huge pyramid of lies which the Catholic and reactionary press all over the world built up'. All of which gave Orwell the 'feeling that the very concept of objective truth is fading out of the world'. MacNeice's retrospect on Spain in *The Strings are False* also fastens on the gap between the perceptions of idealistic or prejudiced outsiders and the actual complexity of the conflict. After rebuking the 'Conservative Press [for] pandering to Franco', he continues:

> The Spanish tragedy ended in fiasco. Miaja, who had long been the hero of the *Daily Worker*, whose statuette was bestowed by the Spanish Ministry of Propaganda on every visitor to Spain, was suddenly covered with pitch as a counter-revolutionary. The young men for whom the Spanish war had been a crusade in white armour, a Quest of the Grail open only to the pure in heart, felt as if their world had burst; there was nothing left but a handful of limp rubber rag; it was no good trying any more. Books such as that by Martin Blazquez, *I Helped to Build an Army*, made only too clear the self-deception which the Civil War had occasioned in nine minds out of ten. There is no such thing as a snow-white cause. The Spanish refugees who began trickling into London surprised Londoners by their retrospective lack of unanimity. (p. 197)

However, that represents wisdom after the event, whereas *Autumn Journal*'s ethic of non-propagandist 'honesty' obliges MacNeice not to alter 'any passages relating to public events in the light of what happened after the time of writing. Thus the section about Barcelona having been written before the fall of Barcelona, I should consider it dishonest to have qualified it retrospectively by my reactions to the later event' (prefatory

Note). There are two sections about Spain in *Autumn Journal.* The first (VI) recalls an immediately pre-war visit with Anthony Blunt: 'And I remember Spain / At Easter ripe as an egg for revolt and ruin'. The second visit, to beleaguered Barcelona (XXIII), takes place in the course of the poem and of the war, after Christmas 1938. MacNeice also chronicles both occasions in *The Strings are False.* In 1937 *Left Review* published a symposium entitled *Authors Take Sides on the Spanish War.* MacNeice's statement belongs to the overwhelming majority which support the legal Republican government against General Franco's Fascist rebellion:

> I support the Valencia government in Spain. Normally I would only support a cause because I hoped to get something out of it. Here the reason is stronger; if this cause is lost, nobody with civilized values may be able to get anything out of anything.

This is among the more temperate pledges in the book (compare 'With all my anger and love, I am for the people of Republican Spain'), not because MacNeice doubted the urgency of fighting Franco but because he doubted his own standing in the matter. 'And I remember Spain' repeats the 'tripper' motif of 'Eclogue from Iceland'. Being a tripper parallels the culpable insulation of middle-class life in Birmingham, even if the protagonist is less directly implicated in the incongruity between 'sherry, shellfish, omelettes' and 'revolt and ruin', than in that between steaks and dole-queues. However, the honesty of *Autumn Journal* consists in laying no claim to greater empathy or comprehension with hindsight, nor to expertise like that of 'a Cambridge don who said with an air / "There's going to be trouble shortly in this country" '. The 'painted hoarding' of Spain, as reproduced in memory, remains faithful to the tripper's 'usual jumble of impressions' (*SAF*, p. 158). At the same time section VI, like all MacNeice's panoramas, reads beneath its own surfaces, especially in the conjunction of the 'shadows of the poor' with 'Monuments of riches or repression'.

'And I remember Spain' seems deliberately understated, as if modifying the sometimes heroic rhetoric of Auden's 'Spain':

On that tableland scored by rivers
Our thoughts have bodies; the menacing shapes of our fever

Are precise and alive . . .

Tomorrow the bicycle races
Through the suburbs on summer evenings. But today the struggle . . .

MacNeice's finale echoes the former quotation, but in a lower key, and with the emphasis still on the lag rather than the coincidence between Spanish and British consciousness:

And next day took the boat
For home, forgetting Spain, not realizing
That Spain would soon denote
Our grief, our aspirations;
Not knowing that our blunt
Ideals would find their whetstone, that our spirit
Would find its frontier on the Spanish front,
Its body in a rag-tag army.

In section XXIII Barcelona acts as a whetstone for blunt ideals, but not in the sense of political enthusiasm. The contrast between this section and section VI typefies the many backwards-and-forwards shuttles of *Autumn Journal*. Instead of prompting guilty retrospect, Spain now presents an alarming prospect: the future shock of 'a place in space where shortly / All of us may be forced to camp in time'. Hungry Barcelona clarifies the painful demands of real war as opposed to the glories of theoretical 'struggle'. In *The Strings are False* MacNeice is ironical about his motives for the journey, and what begins as in part 'sensation-hunting' ends as self-hatred. Similarly, in section XXIII the 'human values . . . purged in the fire' of Barcelona rebuke indifference elsewhere. These values include the survival of individuality:

They breathe the air of war and yet the tension
Admits, beside the slogans it evokes,
An interest in philately or pelota
Or private jokes.

Just as Orwell in *Homage to Catalonia* sees Spain as a violent reproach to the 'deep sleep' of England, so MacNeice's refrain of a crowing cock proclaims the need to wake up, and to admit the voice of conscience: 'the sour / Reproach of Simon Peter'.

The 'cock crowing in Barcelona' brings to a climax *Autumn Journal*'s interweaving of private and public conscience. 'Criticism' is both an important value in the poem, and an agent of its didactic aims: 'I trust that it contains some "criticism of life" or implies some standards which are not merely personal' (prefatory Note). One danger of war is that it suppresses criticism:

> And we who have been brought up to think of 'Gallant Belgium'
>   As so much blague
> Are now preparing again to essay good through evil
>   For the sake of Prague;
> And must, we suppose, become uncritical, vindictive,
>   And must, in order to beat
> The enemy, model ourselves upon the enemy,
>   A howling radio for our paraclete. (VII)

Here MacNeice quotes a propagandist slogan of the First World War, now exploded as 'blague' (nonsense), but likely to have successors. Accordingly he makes the poem a warning against the two 'musts' in that passage, thus acting as Grigson's 'critical moralist'. Satire is the sharpest form of critical moralizing in *Autumn Journal*, whether the irony of section IX ('It was all so unimaginably different / And all so long ago'), or the invective of section XVI ('Scholars and saints my eye'). Section XV satirizes by means of fantasy and nightmare. The appearance of bogeys from the personal and political unconscious is prefaced by an escapist extravaganza like 'Bagpipe Music':

>   Let the critical sense go out and the Roaring Boys come in.
> Give me a houri but houris are too easy,
>   Give me a nun;
> We'll rape the angels off the golden reredos
>   Before we're done.

Besides being satirical, this once again both dramatizes MacNeice's psyche and poses the political alternatives of escapism or engagement. (In fact it points towards the Irish section and the speculation about 'men of action'.) The 'critical sense' of *Autumn Journal* carries conviction because it targets both the self and society, because the protagonist speaks as guilty Everyman and not as preacher or omniscient judge. Hynes classifies the poem, along with other works of the period, under 'Literature of Preparation' (or 'Waiting for the end'). To criticize the past is to prepare for the future. Whereas *in* the past:

> Nobody niggled, nobody cared,
> The soul was deaf to the mounting debit,
> The soul was unprepared. (VIII)

The term *laissez-faire* noticeably recurs throughout *Autumn Journal*, and it covers economic, political and moral sins of omission. Outworn modes of thought as well as of behaviour contribute to *laissez-faire*. The example which might hit at right-wing mental habits is the processing of history to flatter the status quo. This represents a false, dead 'humanism', inimical to the true spirit which *Autumn Journal* redefines. But if MacNeice dislikes the status quo, he distrusts 'the mere Utopia'. His Oxford philosophers might be irrelevant left-wing intellectuals, including MacNeice himself:

> But certainly it was fun while it lasted
> And I got my honours degree
> And was stamped as a person of intelligence and culture
> For ever wherever two or three
> Persons of intelligence and culture
> Are gathered together in talk
> Writing definitions on invisible blackboards
> In non-existent chalk. (XIII)

In *The Strings are False* he compares the 1930s intelligentsia to intellectuals under the Roman Empire who 'spent their time practising rhetoric although they would never use it for any practical purpose' (p. 145). The impulse behind MacNeice's criticism is always to confront abstract or evasive formulations with the real messiness of life, just as at school:

The Fool among the yes-men flashed his motley
To prick their pseudo-reason with his rhymes . . . (X)

If section I establishes *Autumn Journal* as a 'panorama', section II establishes it as 'a confession of faith'. This concentrated soliloquy introduces most subdivisions of MacNeice's persona ('the defeatist, the sensual man, the philosopher, the would-be good citizen'). They interact in a drama which echoes Hamlet's conflict 'To be or not to be'. It thus takes to a new pitch, or to a culmination, the questions of commitment that have agitated the 1930s:

I wonder now whether anything is worth
The eyelid opening and the mind recalling.
And I think of Persephone gone down to dark,
No more a virgin, gone the garish meadow,
But why must she come back, why must the snowdrop mark
That life goes on for ever?
. . .
If you can equate Being in its purest form
With denial of all appearance,
Then let me disappear – the scent grows warm
For pure Not-Being, Nirvana.

The drama will have many issues later on, but the humanistic credo ultimately attained in section II remains crucial to the poem's dynamic:

I must go out tomorrow as the others do
And build the falling castle;
Which has never fallen, thanks
Not to any formula, red tape or institution,
Not to any creeds or banks,
But to the human animal's endless courage.

Setbacks like the end of the affair (XI, XIX) or the Oxford defeat do not permanently frustrate the effort to evolve 'thrust and pattern' i.e. to conceive personal and social integration, and integration between the personal and social. Thus section XXIV imagines, beyond war, a Utopia which would harness individual energies to collective purposes:

a possible land
Not of sleep-walkers, not of angry puppets,
But where both heart and brain can understand
The movements of our fellows;
Where life is a choice of instruments and none
Is debarred his natural music,
Where the waters of life are free of the ice-blockade of hunger
And thought is free as the sun . . .

Its status as a long-term 'dream' may save this Utopia from 'mereness'.

The word that negotiates the final conjunctions of *Autumn Journal* is the lullaby mantra 'sleep'. It accords with MacNeice's deepest symbolic imprinting that a lullaby should counterpoint the insomnia and nightmare of other sections:

Sleep, my body, sleep, my ghost,
Sleep, my parents and grand-parents,
And all those I have loved most.
. . .
Sleep quietly, Marx and Freud,
The figure-heads of our transition.
Cagney, Lombard, Bing and Garbo,
Sleep in your world of celluloid.

The 'natural music' of section XXIV itself not only invokes sleep as a healer, but ends the seasonal and diurnal symbolism of *Autumn Journal* on a positive note. In place of autumn and winter, of 'Persephone gone down to dark', there are redemptive hints of spring and summer. These include sun as opposed to ice-blockades, the wish that MacNeice's divorced wife may 'wake to a glitter of dew and to bird-song', the organic connection between his dead Sligo forefathers and his son: 'A sapling springs in a new country'. And an allusion to 'Snow' suggests transition to a new creative season for the poet himself:

Sleep, my past and all my sins,
In distant snow or dried roses . . .

But the symbolism, like the Utopianism, remains in the optative mood as part of a continuing dialectic between ideal and real. This last historical and autobiographical round-up (which has something in common with 'Last Will and Testament') preserves the poem's open-ended inspiration: 'It is the nature of this poem to be neither final nor balanced' (prefatory Note). MacNeice imposes no artificial stasis on his still fluid materials, including his 'various and conflicting / Selves', but implies that 'preparation' is as complete as it will ever be:

> The New Year comes with bombs, it is too late
>   To dose the dead with honourable intentions.
> . . .
>   Tonight we sleep
> On the banks of Rubicon – the die is cast;
>   There will be time to audit
> The accounts later, there will be sunlight later
>   And the equation will come out at last.

Yet obviously the copious flux of *Autumn Journal* achieves formal finality. Those concluding images resolve even as they postpone. MacNeice's last resort to panoramic method enables him to leave the poem in a state of both aesthetic equilibrium and historical transit. He has been profoundly true to the highest motivation of the thirties writer in that he has discovered structures which betray neither history nor art.

IV
'This Second War'

In 1941, MacNeice wrote five 'London Letters' for the American journal *Common Sense*. Among his subjects were: fire, the morning after air raids, the effect of the war on politics, and 'Blackouts, Bureaucracy and Courage'. The letters sound oddly exhilarated. During the war MacNeice worked for the BBC, making features programmes which were part of the war effort, and served as a fire-watcher. (His eyesight had frustrated an attempt to join the navy.) He published two collections of poems: *Plant and Phantom* (1941) and *Springboard* (1944), now sections VI and VII of the *Collected Poems*. ('Plurality', 'The Casualty' and 'The Kingdom' appear in Section IX.) Section VIII, the bulk of *Holes in the Sky* (1948), contains some poems written in 1944–5 and several retrospects on what he calls in 'Hiatus' 'the years that did not count':

> Yes, we wake stiff and older; especially when
> The schoolboys of the Thirties reappear,
> Fledged in the void, indubitably men,
> Having kept vigil on the Unholy Mount
> And found some dark and tentative things made clear,
> Some clear made dark, in the years that did not count.

The schoolboys of the 1930s, whom the war has matured, might be a metaphor for the Left intelligentsia which, MacNeice remarks in one London Letter, 'broke up in August and September 1939 and all the King's Spitfires and all the King's men have failed to reassemble it'. But the 'void' of the war years was a growth point for him too, and for his poetry.

Nevertheless, the first phase of MacNeice's engagement with the war was a phase of indecision. 'Prognosis', written a few months before September 1939, begins with yet another omen

('The tea-leaf in the teacup / Is herald of a stranger') and then turns into a series of questions:

> What will be his message –
> War or work or marriage?
> News as new as dawn
> Or an old adage?

Even when war at least was certain, the last poem in 'The Closing Album' followed the same format (see page 25). Its final question concerns the relative claims of love and war:

> And why, now it has happened,
> And doom all night is lapping at the door,
> Should I remember that I ever met you –
> Once in another world?

In spring 1939, during a lecture-tour of the USA, MacNeice had fallen in love with Eleanor Clark. Their relationship (celebrated in 'Meeting Point') led him to apply for leave of absence from Bedford College, and in January 1940 he departed to spend a year in America. Meanwhile, however, he had passed the last few months of 1939 'hanging around in [Ireland] communing with my conscience', as he wrote to Dodds. The much-criticized migration of Auden and Isherwood to America in January 1939, over which Dodds had remonstrated with Auden, was probably one factor in MacNeice's self-communing. On the side of keeping out of the war were: love, reluctance to be conscripted for propaganda work (the inevitable fate of intellectuals), and doubts as to whether the war would lead anywhere: 'It is all very well for everyone to go on saying "Destroy Hitlerism" but what the hell are they going to construct?' A later letter to Dodds puts the positive case:

> My conscience is troubling me about this fool war. I am beginning to think this may be *my* war after all. It doesn't seem any good being perfectionist like the Trotskyites & E[leanor] over in America. Obviously there is plenty wrong with the British Empire & especially India & no doubt our present Government have no intention of mending this state of affairs. However the war they are supposed to be running may mend it in spite of them. I find myself liable to use things like India or

> interferences with liberty at home to rationalize my own cowardice. It does however seem to be clear that, in this choice of evils, Mr Chamberlain's England is preferable to Nazi Germany (& anyhow it won't, if people have sense, remain Mr C.'s England.)

While in America MacNeice formulated 'a new attitude, the basic principle of which is that Freedom means Getting Into things & not Getting Out of them' (letter to Dodds). 'Traveller's Return', an article in *Horizon* (February 1941), implicitly reflects this philosophy, but also deprecates his reasons for returning – much as he had deprecated his visit to Barcelona:

> You cannot forget the War in America (it is the chief subject of conversation), but you cannot visualize it. I could visualize it myself so long as the 'Sitzkrieg' [Phoney War] persisted, and during that period I had no wish to return to a Chamberlain's England, where my fellow-writers were sitting around not writing. From June on I wished to return, not because I thought I could be more *useful* in England than in America, but because I wanted to see these things for myself. My chief motive thus being vulgar curiosity, my second motive was no less egotistical: I thought that if I stayed another year out of England I should have to stay out for good, having missed so much history, lost touch.

'Traveller's Return' vigorously defends Auden, Isherwood and other expatriate writers: 'The expatriates do not need anybody else to act as their *ersatz* conscience: they have consciences of their own and the last word must be said by their own instinct as artists.' MacNeice emphasizes that being 'more attached to things than to ideas', whereas the reverse is true of Auden, he has simply followed his own artistic instinct back to England and the Blitz. A comment to Mrs Dodds suggests, like the London Letters, that his sense of direction has proved accurate: 'We play Rummy here [at the BBC] every night. It occurs to me that even playing Rummy in London now is a kind of assertion of the Rights of Man, whereas in America it would be nothing but playing Rummy.'

Plant and Phantom, in some respects a sixth act of *Autumn Journal*, vibrates with the tension between getting into things and getting out of them. After 'Prognosis' comes 'Stylite' (March 1940) which stylizes this renewed problem of choice. An introspective saint on a pillar in the desert 'bans' the world until 'Round his neck there comes / The conscience of a rope'. (The word 'conscience' recurs in the letters to Dodds.) On the opposite pillar stands a confident 'Greek god' with 'his eyes on the world'. Between these pillars MacNeice strings broad metaphysical issues cxplored in such poems as 'Entirely', 'Plant and Phantom', 'London Rain', and 'Plurality' (see chapter VI). 'Entirely' examines the decision-making process itself, concluding that 'in brute reality there is no / Road that is right entirely'. MacNeice has thus felt impelled to reopen the old question of the universe – 'Plant and Phantom' tackles the question head on – a universe which war is now helping to churn into worse than flux: 'a mad weir of tigerish waters'. But he also specifically reopens the question of responsibility which so troubles *Autumn Journal*, and which has been all along, perhaps, his version of 'commitment'. Some poems with this slant, all written in America, are: 'Débâcle', 'Flight of the Heart', 'Bar-room Matins', 'Jehu' and 'Evening in Connecticut'. 'Débâcle' elaborates the 'falling castle' of *Autumn Journal*, but here the 'heirs' of civilization have betrayed the builders whose 'Vision and sinew made it of light and stone'. In 'Flight of the Heart', a miniature drama of self-division, MacNeice 'the would-be good citizen' interrogates one unworthy heir: MacNeice 'the defeatist'. The speaker who persists in evading the 'demands' of humanity and its general crisis, has ultimately no refuge but non-being:

> But what when the cellar roof caves in
> With one blue flash and nine old bones?
> How, my heart, will you save your skin?
>
>   I will go back where I belong
>   With one foot first and both eyes blind
>   I will go back where I belong
>   In the fore-being of mankind.

If we reverse the irony, 'go back where I belong' seems to enlarge Grettir's admonition at the end of 'Eclogue from Iceland'. 'Flight of the Heart' was written in October 1940. Only 'Cradle Song for

Eleanor' shares so late a date, and this poem reads like a valediction as well as a benediction. It may be significant that MacNeice *did* date all the poems in *Plant and Phantom* (a practice he had not adopted in *The Earth Compels*). To be conscious of dates is to be conscious of history.

Throughout MacNeice's poetry the 'golden seas of drink' ('Alcohol') supply metaphors for moral evasion. The final kick of 'Night Club' (from 'Entered in the Minutes'), written in autumn 1939, is 'Salome comes in, bearing / The head of God knows whom'. Nine months later 'Bar-room Matins' switches the scene to America ('Pretzels crackers chips and beer') and renders it as an ironic liturgy:

> Mass destruction, mass disease:
> We thank thee, Lord, upon our knees
> That we were born in times like these
>
> When with doom tumbling from the sky
> Each of us has an alibi
> For doing nothing – Let him die.

Using fatalism as an excuse for escapism, this chorus refuses to be 'My brother's keeper'. Here MacNeice combines self-criticism with criticism of America's isolationist stance, and prophetically attacks the conversion of suffering into a media event:

> Die the soldiers, die the Jews,
> And all the breadless homeless queues.
> Give us this day our daily news.

'Jehu' and 'Evening in Connecticut' are also preoccupied with distances from reality. They begin by evoking idyllic American summer and autumn landscapes which, like the Irish environments of 'The Closing Album', represent 'outmoded peace'. (In 'Traveller's Return' MacNeice says: 'in America I felt a very long way from Europe, though not so far away as I felt during the autumn of 1939 in Ireland'.) After its pastoral first stanza 'Jehu' turns an Old Testament story into a parable which raises similar issues to 'Stylite'. The king whose chariot wheels destroy Jezebel personifies the momentum of war: irresistible but strangely meaningless, since he has lived in the desert with the 'deceiving / Mirage of what were once ideals or even motives'. The narrator's relation to Jehu's frenzy remains problematic:

And now the sand blows over Kent and Wales where we may
shortly
Learn the secret of the desert's purge, of the mad driving,
The cautery of the gangrened soul, though we are not certain
Whether we shall stand beside
The charioteer, the surgeon, or shall be one with the pampered
Queen who tittered in the face of death, unable to imagine
The meaning of the flood tide.

This does not greet war as a necessary purgation, whether in the spirit of 1914 or of 1930. However, the 'meaning' seems to be that the world affords no sanctuary or sanction against 'the flood tide'. Similarly in 'Evening in Connecticut' 'Nature is not to be trusted', and the contemplator of falling leaves finds them inseparable from 'The fall of dynasties; the emergence / Of sleeping kings from caves'. The poem's refrain, 'Only the shadows longer and longer', stresses that there is finally no freedom for free lances in this American garden either.

Not only 'Jehu' but most of the poems so far discussed can be called 'parables'. They have not undergone the full technical revolution of MacNeice's later parables (see chapter V), but they combine emblematic and moral elements in various ways. *Plant and Phantom* marks the beginning of his dissatisfaction with journalism, with panoramas, with 'chunks of life'. The London Letters of 1941 were to indicate what a brilliant war correspondent MacNeice might have been. Perhaps radio work, like prose, siphoned off his documentary impulses (and some of his didactic impulses into the dreaded propaganda). But a bad journalistic poem, 'Refugees', suggests that he was near the end of one aesthetic tether, or that certain thirties methods had become obsolete: 'With prune-dark eyes, thick lips, jostling each other . . .' In 'Experiences with Images' MacNeice cites poems from *Plant and Phantom* and *Springboard* to illustrate his new 'structural type of image' (*SCLM*, p. 162). He mentions 'The Springboard', which complements 'Stylite' as a parable of choice.

Two years on, the relatively abstract and static scenario of the earlier poem has been invaded by images and emotions of war:

> And yet we know he knows what he must do.
> There above London where the gargoyles grin
> He will dive like a bomber past the broken steeple,
> One man wiping out his own original sin
> And, like ten million others, dying for the people.

Some chunks of life survive in *Plant and Phantom*, though not in a documentary form. The sequence 'Novelettes' gathers together under an ironic title several stories of MacNeice's own life. These poems are more about facing the past than about facing the future; but the two processes converge as a struggle against cosy fictions. 'Novelettes' only marginally refers to war or prospects of war. Yet in developing the autobiographical strand of *Autumn Journal* the poems enter psychological and moral areas which ultimately belong to a single 'tigerish' universe. MacNeice's wartime poetry in one sense separates what *Autumn Journal* joins; in another sense reunites it at a further point. 'The Gardener' (see page 17) is the only happy novelette. It may be ominous that the old man's happiness depends on his not being '*quite all there*', although his eccentricity rebukes so-called sanity. 'Christina' resurrects a less benign childhood memory. A broken doll becomes an image of disillusionment and sexual betrayal: 'her legs and arms were hollow / And her yellow head was hollow'. This poem, 'The Old Story', 'Les Sylphides' and 'Provence' evidently originated as post mortems on MacNeice's first marriage. 'Christina', parable rather than chunk of life, is his most powerful version of its doll's-house unreality:

> He went to bed with a lady
> Somewhere seen before,
> He heard the name Christina
> And suddenly saw Christina
> Dead on the nursery floor.

As in some of his later poems, MacNeice exploits the buried violence of the nursery and the nursery rhyme. 'The Old Story' – 'The old story is true of charms fading' – also explores, less shockingly but no less painfully, changed perceptions of a female image. An agonizing truth resides in the mature knowledge that not just other people's charms but one's own feelings can fade: 'he found the difference / A surgeon's knife without an anaesthetic'. 'Provence' ironically measures difference by making the indifference of old age a comment on young love and 'perfect happiness':

> . . . he suddenly said
> 'We must get married soon.' Down on the beach,
> His wife and three of his three children dead,
> An old man lay in the sun, perfectly happy.

'Les Sylphides' must be one of the best poems ever written on marriage:

> So they were married – to be the more together –
> And found they were never again so much together,
> Divided by the morning tea,
> By the evening paper,
> By children and tradesmen's bills.
>
> Waking at times in the night she found assurance
> In his regular breathing but wondered whether
> It was really worth it and where
> The river had flowed away
> And where were the white flowers.

The poem's imagery of dancing, music, movement, flowers and water recalls 'Mayfly'; but here the dream of eternal togetherness ends up under a changed sky.

All the novelettes are elegies or epitaphs. They conclude with vistas of death or change, with more decisive endings than those of 1938. Only 'The Gardener' envisages a happy ending, and this is consciously a fairy-tale one. The symbol which ends 'The Old Story' blends emotional disorientation with the arrival of a warlike future: 'he . . . watched the water / Massing for action on the cold horizon'. A warmer obituary, 'Death of an Actress', also connects the elegiac strain in *Plant and Phantom* with its historical context. The death of the music-hall artiste Florrie Forde, which occurred while MacNeice was in America, inspires his most sumptuous imagery of performance:

Plush and cigars; she waddled into the lights,
Old and huge and painted, in velvet and tiara,
Her voice gone but around her head an aura
Of all her vanilla-sweet forgotten vaudeville nights.

With an elephantine shimmy and a sugared wink
She threw a trellis of Dorothy Perkins roses
Around an audience come from slum and suburb
And weary of the tea-leaves in the sink;

Who found her songs a rainbow leading west
To the home they never had, to the chocolate Sunday
Of boy and girl, to cowslip time, to the never-
Ending weekend Islands of the Blest.

Over-sweet, over-coloured, over the top, these impressions for once indulge escape – at least from the social constraints of 'slum and suburb' and marriage. But Florrie Forde's career also spans war, against which her anodynes are less effective:

In the Isle of Man before the war before
The present one she made a ragtime favourite
Of 'Tipperary', which became the swan-song
Of troop-ships on a darkened shore;

And during Munich sang her ancient quiz
Of *Where's Bill Bailey?* and the chorus answered,
Muddling through and glad to have no answer:
Where's Bill Bailey? How do *we* know where he is!

Altogether 'Death of an Actress' (which should be a better-known poem) marvellously distils the belated end of an era, of 'an older England'. It forgives the innocence if not the ignorance of that England, which had followed 'Tipperary' to doom and been 'glad to have no answer' to Munich. The finale is another of MacNeice's benedictions, but partly so because it is definitively a finale:

Now on a late and bandaged April day
In a military hospital Miss Florrie
Forde has made her positively last appearance
And taken her bow and gone correctly away.

Correctly. For she stood
For an older England, for children toddling
Hand in hand while the day was bright. Let the wren and robin
Gently with leaves cover the Babes in the Wood.

'Death of an Actress' stands to MacNeice's outer world as 'The Gardener' to his inner history. Both poems reserve happiness to age, illusion and a receding past. But the association of these old people with eternal youth simultaneously dramatizes a farewell to childhood on MacNeice's part. The death of 'Babes in the Wood' marks a break with former psychological and social conditions.

Springboard begins not with prognosis but with prayer. In 'Prayer before Birth' the world of 1944 reaches even into the womb:

I am not yet born, console me.
I fear that the human race may with tall walls wall me,
with strong drugs dope me, with wise lies lure me,
on black racks rack me, in blood-baths roll me . . .

I am not yet born; O hear me,
Let not the man who is beast or who thinks he is God
come near me.

'Prayer before Birth' seems to me an overrated poem: too routinely chosen by anthologists to represent the darker MacNeice, as 'Bagpipe Music' is too routinely chosen to represent his lighter side. But perhaps its somewhat melodramatic rhetoric should be understood as a product of 1944, and as a series of headlines for the poems that follow. Like war, the perspective of the unborn highlights the powerful imperatives which mock our belief in individual autonomy. These imperatives vary from the predetermined ('the sins that in me the world shall commit') to the totalitarian:

I am not yet born; O fill me
With strength against those who would freeze my
humanity, would dragoon me into a lethal automaton,
would make me a cog in a machine, a thing with
one face, a thing, and against all those
who would dissipate my entirety . . .

Resistance to such pressures is still humanistically conceived. The unborn individual pins his hopes of 'humanity' and 'entirety' on a kindly Nature ('water to dandle me') and the light of reason invested with spiritual authority: 'a white light / in the back of my mind to guide me'. 'Prayer before Birth' resembles some of the parables of *Plant and Phantom* in so far as it takes an archetypal view of contemporary struggles. It exposes the instincts and processes that lie beneath politics, as Auden in 'September 1, 1939' ponders 'What huge imago made / A psychopathic god'. Earlier in the war MacNeice had defended 'make-believe' and 'fantasy' on the grounds that 'in the epoch of Hitler – Siegfried Redivivus – it is not only a mistake but a disaster to ignore those underground motives which cause both art and war' (*SAF*, p. 77). Thus 'Prayer before Birth' begins with folk-lore images which suggest the monsters lurking in our collective unconscious: 'Let not the bloodsucking bat . . . or the club-footed ghoul come near me.'

'Brother Fire', 'The Trolls' and 'Troll's Courtship' psycho-analyse the Blitz by personifying fire and bombing as mythical creatures. In one of his London Letters MacNeice admits to a voyeuristic fascination with the spectacle of fire:

> I had never before realized the infinite variety of fire – subtleties never attained by any Impressionist painter. These fires were a wedding of power with a feminine sensuous beauty. A glowering crimson power mottled with black; a yellow liquid power – a kind of Virgin Birth – which is sheer destruction; a crackling, a hissing, and an underground growling. But up above were the softest clouds of smoke – soft as marabou – purple and umber and pink and orange which spread out and shade off to blue.

The title of 'Brother Fire' suggests an unholy kinship between man and the destructive forces he has unleashed. Fire, 'having his dog's day', acts out elemental energies which are always latent in man as well as in Nature, and which may make wars inevitable. The poem ends:

> O delicate walker, babbler, dialectician Fire,
> O enemy and image of ourselves,
> Did we not on those mornings after the All Clear,

When you were looting shops in elemental joy
And singing as you swarmed up city block and spire,
Echo your thought in ours? 'Destroy! Destroy!'

The first line of that stanza shows that MacNeice has not dropped his association between the destructive urge and the manipulation of language. In 'Prayer before Birth' a propaganda corps awaits the infant: 'wise lies', 'the cues I must take when / old men lecture me, bureaucrats hector me'. The parable poem 'Babel' ('There was a tower that went before a fall') blames mutually unintelligible languages for the collapsing world:

Patriots, dreamers, die-hards, theoreticians, all,
Can't we ever, my love, speak in the same language,
Or shall we go, still quarrelling over words, to the wall?
Have we no aims in common?

'The Trolls' escalates the relation between propaganda and apocalypse into a bombardment of meaningless noise: 'humming to themselves like morons'. The sound and fury of the Blitz give MacNeice's onomatopoeia a grim licence: 'They ramble and rumble over the roof-tops, stumble and shamble from pile to pillar'. However, the conclusion challenges 'Silence of men and trolls' triumph' and 'Troll's Courtship' starts from the premiss that trolls are 'Wrong, wrong in the end'. Here 'a lonely Troll' speaks for himself, for the monstrous mutation of humanity feared in 'Prayer before Birth', for destruction as the inverse of poetry, for the neurotic unconscious of total war, for its self-defeating logic: 'My lusts and lonelinesses grunt and heave / And blunder round among the ruins that I leave.' 'The Streets of Laredo' in *Holes in the Sky* presents the Blitz, 'the voice of the fire', in a folk-song rather than a folk-lore idiom. Like 'Bagpipe Music' this ballad combines a traditional rhythm with surreal images. However, it also marks some mutations in London and in MacNeice's poetry since *Autumn Journal*:

Then out from a doorway there sidled a cockney,
A rocking-chair rocking on top of his head:
'O fifty-five years I been feathering my love-nest
And look at it now – why, you'd sooner be dead.'

As well as interpreting war by means of fantastic archetypal patterns, MacNeice absorbs some of its realistic images into his own patterns. 'Convoy', 'Bottleneck' and 'The Conscript' are (like 'Neutrality') moralities of the human condition which derive from wartime circumstances. 'Convoy' seems not only to recognize a neat emblem but to imply that war has enforced its recognition:

> This is a bit like us: the individual sets
> A course for all his soul's more basic needs
> Of love and pride-of-life, but sometimes he forgets
> How much their voyage home depends upon pragmatic
> And ruthless attitudes – destroyers and corvettes.

'Bottleneck' complements 'Convoy' in that it characterizes the theorist who baulks at 'pragmatic and ruthless attitudes'. This poem reads like a portrait of the divided but unreconstructed 1930s intellectual: 'Who had been in books and visions to a progressive school / And dreamt of barricades'. Now, however, 'The permanent bottleneck of his highmindedness' prevents him from being truly 'combined / Into a working whole'. The latter is MacNeice's old ideal of community, which he himself partly realized in the wartime BBC (see Barbara Coulton, *Louis MacNeice in the BBC*, chapter 3). That 'Convoy' and 'Bottleneck' value pragmatism, facts and co-operative work suggests too how the spirit of the times suited MacNeice's preference of things to ideas. But 'things' now means empiricism, i.e. starting from a given situation, rather than social realism. A reflective essay, 'Broken Windows or Thinking Aloud', probably written in 1941, brings together some of the ideas behind *Springboard*. 'Broken Windows' relates changes in MacNeice's writing to a changed environment and ethos. It is his most important formulation of an aesthetic – or even a theology – of 'war poetry', one distinctively shaped by his experiences in London:

> Not that my primary concern at the moment is writing. Whoso at the moment saveth his art shall lose it . . .
>
> The 'message' of a work of art may appear to be defeatist, negative, nihilist; the work of art itself is always *positive*. A poem in praise of suicide is an act of homage to life.

But different circumstances change the 'message' – the content – and so the method – the style. I notice myself that my two old methods – reportage and lyric – are ceasing to suit me. And I notice I have lost my nostalgia, am no longer worried by the passage of time . . .

'The best lack all conviction and the worst
Are full of passionate intensity'.

These lines of Yeats remain the classic description of the last twenty years.

Oh, I know in the 'Thirties the boys ran after conviction; they wrote high-minded poetry, they sat on high-minded committees. But High-Mindedness isn't conviction; it is like Self-Respect – a rather frowsy cul-de-sac.

Now the bombs have broken the end wall . . .

Some of us go jingo and some of us go religious – muzzily religious with a great deal of hand-washing. And some of us try to remain where we were – high-minded nineteenth century liberals (liberals in spite of a flirtation with Marx and Victorian in spite of – or because of? – our cult of the Future) . . .

But isn't it a pity if you have to choose between the Astral Plane and High-Mindedness? Aren't there other choices?

'Empiricism?' You say that rather scornfully; it depends on what you mean by it. An 'empiricist' may be someone who lives from hand to mouth. Or he may be someone who follows an ideal that is always developing, implicit rather than explicit.

'The Conscript' also originates in this set of ideas. 'Conscription' makes an apt metaphor for historical necessity:

Being so young he feels the weight of history
Like clay around his boots; he would, if he could, fly
In search of a future like a sycamore seed
But is prevented by his own Necessity,
His own yet alien, which, whatever he may plead,
To every question gives the same reply.

Yet the two-dimensional 'groove' of history can be counteracted by a three-dimensional humanity: by 'life's largesse', by the fact that man's 'inward stalk / Vertically aspires and makes him his own master' and links him with both the earth and the stars. This accords with the statement in 'Broken Windows' that: 'Today we are all being dragooned by outside conditions, we look like the shuttlecocks of War. It is therefore all the more necessary to think of ourselves as free agents.' Some poems in *Springboard* celebrate free agents. (Even the figure in the title poem is not quite conscripted.) 'Precursors' models redemptive people on MacNeice's life-affirming imagery of movement, water, colour and light. It is grouped with 'Explorations' and 'Mutations' whose very titles also defy necessity and anticipate a future:

> For every static word that you or I impose
> Upon the real one must crack at times and new
> Patterns from new disorders open like a rose
> And old assumptions yield to new sensation;
> The Stranger in the wings is waiting for his cue,
> The fuse is always laid to some annunciation.
> ('Mutations')

Here flux and MacNeice's faith in 'surprise' defeat the wartime version of stasis and petrifaction. This prospective stranger is not the figure who haunts 'Prognosis'. More elaborately, 'The Kingdom' consists of character sketches of people (including MacNeice's recently dead father) who have escaped the groove, 'who have the courage / Of their own vision and their friends' goodwill'. The ideal of 'the Kingdom of individuals' remains an ideal, or at best 'an underground movement'. But 'The Kingdom', although far from entirely successful, reflects the communal experience of war in putting more flesh on the Utopian theme of *Autumn Journal*, and in conveying greater urgency than MacNeice's post-war praise of his friends in *Autumn Sequel*. 'The Casualty', also a rather sprawling poem in comparison with the sinewy parables, commemorates another candidate for the Kingdom: Graham Shepard, MacNeice's friend since Marlborough days, who was killed in the North Atlantic (hence perhaps the bitterness of 'Neutrality'). Like all elegies for creative people – compare Yeats's 'In Memory of Major Robert Gregory' – 'The Casualty' also throws light on its author's aesthetic. In the best passages Shepard's hyper-individuality exaggerates the 'homage to life' at the core of MacNeice's wartime poetry, its refusal to be overpowered by a context of darkness and grief:

> For you were a good mixer and could laugh
> With Rowlandson or Goya and you liked
> Bijoux and long-eared dogs and silken legs
> And titivated rooms but more than half
> Your story lay outside beyond the spiked
> Railing where in the night the blinded minstrel begs . . .

'Broken Windows' ends with MacNeice's most profound account of war as an experience and as an aesthetic:

> Death in its own right – as War does incidentally – sets our lives in perspective. Every man's funeral is his own, just as people are lonely in their lives, but Death as a leveller also unites us in life. And death not only levels but differentiates – it crystallizes our deeds.
>
> We did not need a war to teach us this but war has taught us it. Before the war we wore blinkers. Applied science, by increasing comfort and controlling disease, had – geared to a 'liberal' individualism – encouraged us to think of death as a pure negation, a nuisance. But applied science, by shattering a town overnight, by superimposing upon ordered decay a fantastic but palpable madness, has shown us the integral function of death. Death is the opposite of decay; a stimulus, a necessary horizon.
>
> And this will affect our conception of Freedom . . .

Several poems written later in the war and after the war come to less absolute conclusions. The ambiguous balance sheet of 'Hiatus' – 'some dark and tentative things made clear, / Some clear made dark' – corresponds to the oscillation between 'The News-Reel' and 'Aftermath'. The former, which begins by asking 'Since Munich, what?', refuses to fabricate a premature journalistic synthesis but finds mutations which point towards 'a rhythm and a meaning'. Among the hopeful signs are 'that sudden unconfined / Wind of understanding that blew out / From people's hands and faces'. 'Aftermath' paradoxically laments 'the bandaging dark which bound / This town together', and sees synthesis as no longer on the cards: 'What was so large and one / Is now a pack of dog's-eared chances.' Class-divisions will resume their sway: 'Their ransomed future severs once more the child / Of luck from the child of lack.' In these poems social and imaginative 'oneness' seem virtually interchangeable concepts. The question is: what understanding, what bonding, what unified vision survives the war? MacNeice is recycling his old conundrums about the individual and society, poetry and society. Some poems in *Springboard* are generic case histories of maladjustment between the self and the group. 'The Mixer', partly due to the 'shadows of a night / In Flanders', represents an extreme of dissolution into the social mass, of dissipated entirety:

> So in this second war which is fearful too,
> He cannot away with silence but has grown
> Almost a cipher, like a Latin word
> That many languages have made their own
> Till it is worn and blunt and easy to construe
> And often spoken but no longer heard.

'The Libertine' – now less free than 'The Conscript' – has paid the price for a different promiscuity. The refrain, 'O leave me easy, leave me alone', hardens as his incapacity for personal relationships becomes chronic. 'The Satirist' chooses loneliness because he over-reacts to society's own chronic lack:

> Who is that man with eyes like a lonely dog?
> Lonely is right. He knows that he has missed
> What others miss unconsciously. Assigned
> To a condemned ship he still must keep the log
> And so fulfil the premises of his mind
> Where large ideals have bred a satirist.

There are elements of MacNeice himself in all three incarnations. However, wartime access to 'a working whole' has given him a point of balance which precludes the disillusioned 'mere Utopianism' of 'The Satirist'. (In 1936 MacNeice had called the satirist 'a kind of escapist'.) But he perceives the balance tilting elsewhere. 'Bluebells' contrasts present social maladjustment with former integration by portraying a relationship which has lost the organic meaning it acquired during the war: 'all green Nature has gone out of gear / Since they were apart and hoping, since last year'. Similarly, most of MacNeice's aftermath poems seem to be in mourning for lost intensities. In the parable 'Twelfth Night' snow's 'unity', reversing its unfavourable image in 'To a Communist', is an object of humorous regret:

> Here is dull earth to build upon
> Undecorated; we have reached
> Twelfth Night or what you will . . . you will.

Once again MacNeice is writing epitaphs and elegies: poems of nostalgia, ending and transition to new choices. 'Epitaph for Liberal Poets' (although published in *Springboard*) might cover the whole stretch of years, the whole literary phase, from 1930 to 1945:

> . . .
> The Individual has died before; Catullus
> Went down young, gave place to those who were born old
> And more adaptable and were not even jealous
> Of his wild life and lyrics. Though our songs
> Were not so warm as his, our fate is no less cold.
>
> Such silence then before us, pinned against the wall,
> Why need we whine? There is no way out, the birds
> Will tell us nothing more; we shall vanish first,
> Yet leave behind us certain frozen words
> Which some day, though not certainly, may melt
> And, for a moment or two, accentuate a thirst.

This epitaph accepts that the world has passed the thirties poets by, or that they bypassed too much of the world. But even while MacNeice acknowledges their historical obsolescence, he claims his share in a lasting artistic if not social synthesis. And he implies that the former at least keeps alive the possibility of the latter.

V
Colour and Meaning

I

MacNeice's writings on poetry are invaluable to the student of his work. They are also important documents in the history of twentieth-century poetry. He began his first extended essay, 'Poetry Today' (1935), by probing the motivation behind a poet's criticism:

> Poets do not know (exactly) what they are doing, for if they did, there would be no need to do it. So much of truth is there in the Plato–Shelley doctrine of Poetic Inspiration. Poetry is not a science and it is more than a craft. This is why, when the poet tries to explain his work, he is much less helpful than the mechanic explaining an engine. But it is a human characteristic that the poet must try to explain and the reader to comprehend why, how and what the poet writes. (*SCLM*, p. 10)

Fifteen years later, however, MacNeice seemed less constructively unsure about what he was doing, and less sure-footed in doing it. The creative crisis he suffered during the late 1940s and early 1950s makes a good vantage point from which to consider the evolution of his aesthetic: i.e. of his poetic theory and technical practice. In 1963, looking over *The Burning Perch*, he could 'see both the continuity and the difference' as compared with 'poems I was writing thirty years ago' (*SCLM*, p. 248). His theory – which usually followed practice, sometimes led it, and never floated abstractly free – can be traced in *Modern Poetry*, *The Poetry of W. B. Yeats*, *Varieties of Parable* and *Selected Literary Criticism of Louis MacNeice*.

MacNeice wrote about poetry neither for an academic audience nor for received opinion: 'The literary critic fails through being literary' (*SCLM*, p. 58). Besides trying to explain his work to others and to himself, he wrote as an evangelist on behalf of his generation and on behalf of poetry in general. One of his consistent themes, not only in the 1930s, is that: 'Given a community, however loose a one, there should not be an unbridgeable gulf between its poets and its readers' (*SCLM*, p. 166). In keeping with his attitude to politics, MacNeice emphasized from the outset not how poetry might help to change society, but how a sense of social obligation might change poetry. That the circumstances of the 1930s placed a premium on 'content' is indicated by the very title of his essay 'Subject in Modern Poetry' (1936), in which he objects to 'literary self-containedness' and argues that 'not only the muck and wind of existence should be faced but also the prose of existence, the utilities, the *sine qua nons*, which are never admitted to the world, or rather the salon, of the Pure Artist.' (*SCLM*, p. 58)

This essay and 'Poetry Today' contributed to the making of *Modern Poetry*, whose opening 'Change of Attitude' chapter draws together their attacks on the 'escape-art' of the nineties poets and Georgian poets. MacNeice measures these earlier movements by the degree of their failure to make the poet 'organic to the community', whereas contemporary poets 'are working back from luxury-writing and trying once more to become functional' (pp. 2–3). Words themselves bring to poetry their status as 'a community-product' and perform within poetry their function as 'a vehicle of communication' (pp. 3–5). MacNeice did not disown these attitudes in the changed literary climates of later years. Reviewing in 1960 a book about Wilfred Owen, a primary model for the thirties poets, he argued:

> Mr Welland dwells on the dangers inherent in Owen's kind of poetry. 'When the motivating feelings are most intense it is likely to become cheaply rhetorical as did so much minor but unquestionably sincere left-wing poetry in the 1930's' (Touché!). 'It has somehow to avoid' he goes on 'the double pitfall of telling the reader about the pity, for that would become sentimentality, and of over-emphasizing the suffering, for that would become painful morbidity.' Yes indeed, there is such a double pitfall but there is a narrow way through and it is still worth trying to walk it. For that is the human way. If you

> take any wide detour you may indeed produce works of art but they will not be so germane to the life of our time.

In the same year he approved of *Over the Bridge*, Sam Thompson's play about sectarianism in the Belfast shipyards, on the following grounds: 'Social consciousness seems to have become, among the younger generation, a dirty phrase, but, when most of our writers are lowering their sights, pulling their punches, drawing in their horns, and generally playing safe, it is very refreshing to encounter a work such as this which reaffirms the eternal commonplaces of the misery – and the dignity – of man.'

By the standards of MacNeice's ideal 'concrete poet' responding as a whole to 'concrete living', even Eliot and Yeats can fail. *Modern Poetry* reveals MacNeice, perhaps due to his Irishness, as the most obsessively genealogical of the thirties poet–critics. Although his long historical perspective is capable of co-opting Homer or Horace into the contemporary argument, he particularly broods (as he does elsewhere) on Eliot and Yeats as the challenging predecessors to be challenged. In 'Poetry Today' he says: 'For me the history of post-War poetry in England is the history of Eliot and the reaction from Eliot' (*SCLM*, p. 39) – a formulation from which Ireland excludes Yeats. *Modern Poetry* gives Eliot due credit for introducing into poetry 'the modern industrial city . . . [and] the background of European history', together with ' "the boredom and glory" of the contemporary world'; but criticizes his 'bookishness', 'defeatism', and the extent to which his poems remain 'studies from a corner' (pp. 11–15). MacNeice sums up the earlier Eliot as 'not a great poet nor essentially a tragic poet, but a very sensitive aesthete in literature, learned in and obsessed with the past, for whom the problem is not the problem of a world-builder or a believer or a rebel or even a reporter, but the problem of a rather pedantic individualist who would like his daily life and his personal relationships to conform to some pattern which he has extracted from other people's poetry or philosophy' (p. 59). The thirties poet has evidently taken on the 'problems' which Eliot disregards.

MacNeice's poetry too pursues this argument. For the most part – at all periods – it comments on its own principles only at a subtextual level. However, the eclogues include poetic theory among their topics for debate. As already noted (see page 45), 'An Eclogue for Christmas' simultaneously imitates and 'reacts from' Eliot. It also justifies the reaction in terms which anticipate MacNeice's judgement of Eliot in *Modern Poetry* as 'bound to be a rather esoteric poet because . . . he really is more interested in ideas on the one hand and sense-impressions on the other – Spinoza and smells – than in concrete life or the concrete human being' (p. 168). In the eclogue 'A' criticizes the course of the century and of the modern movement, using abstract art as an inclusive metaphor for progressive dehumanization:

> I who was Harlequin in the childhood of the century,
> Posed by Picasso beside an endless opaque sea,
> Have seen myself sifted and splintered in broken facets,
> Tentative pencillings, endless liabilities, no assets,
> Abstractions scalpelled with a palette-knife
> Without reference to this particular life.
> And so it has gone on; I have not been allowed to be
> Myself in flesh or face, but abstracting and dissecting me
> They have made of me pure form, a symbol or a pastiche,
> Stylized profile, anything but soul and flesh . . .

Aestheticism (Art for Art's sake) and Modernism, which partly descends from it, have denied and fragmented man's concrete wholeness. Even if the poem's own posture largely acquiesces in this condition, it is significant for MacNeice's aesthetic that the speaker prefers fleshly particularities to abstractions, symbolism, and 'pure form'.

In 'Poetry Today' MacNeice finds Yeats less esoteric than Eliot in some respects, more so in others. Yeats scores in that the Irish Literary Revival was 'healthily mixed up with politics' and 'Where it is possible to be a hypocrite, it is also possible to be a hero, a saint, or an artist' (*SCLM*, p. 15). *Modern Poetry*, perhaps because more a manifesto than a survey, is harder on Yeats as a poet of the library, but still acknowledges that 'through identifying himself with the Irish nationalist movement, [he] had to recognize the palpable realities of living people and contemporary problems' (p. 10). It might be said that 'Eclogue from Iceland' applies and redefines aspects of Yeats's aesthetic, as 'An Eclogue for Christmas' comes to terms with Eliot's. *Modern Poetry* is more inconsistent on Yeats than on Eliot, probably because MacNeice's quarrels with him have a deeper cultural basis. He does not really reconcile the Yeatsian poles of esotericism and public involvement. It took a full-length study to get Yeats into perspective, and it also took the atmosphere of autumn 1939. Whereas *Modern Poetry* was partly shaped by the Spanish Civil War and impending crisis, *The Poetry of W. B. Yeats*, like *Plant and Phantom*, was partly shaped by the coming of war. It opens in the spirit of 'The Closing Album':

> As soon as I heard on the wireless of the outbreak of war, Galway became unreal. And Yeats and his poetry became unreal also.
>
> This was not merely because Galway and Yeats belong in a sense to a past order of things. The unreality which now overtook them was also overtaking in my mind modern London, modernist art, and Left Wing politics. If the war made nonsense of Yeats's poetry and of all works that are called 'escapist', it also made nonsense of the poetry that professes to be 'realist'. My friends had been writing for years about guns and frontiers and factories, about the 'facts' of psychology, politics, science, economics, but the fact of war made their writing seem as remote as the pleasure dome in Xanadu. For war spares neither the poetry of Xanadu nor the poetry of pylons. (pp. 17–18)

Two related realignments in MacNeice's thinking about poetry now bring him closer to Yeats. Firstly, he feels that in *Modern Poetry* 'I over-stressed the half-truth that poetry is *about* something, is communication' (p. 15). Secondly, Yeats now appears less 'mannered' in comparison with Eliot due to MacNeice's recognition that 'Eliot's poetry itself is largely both mannerism and fantasy and that the daylight of "realism" is itself largely a fiction' (p. 122). And overall, because he has revised his concept of 'escapism', MacNeice can detect in Yeats's poetry, below the levels of subject matter and ideology, impulses which unite him in spirit with the thirties 'school of poets':

> Eliot . . . had maintained that the poet must adapt himself to his world; if his world is difficult and complex, his poetry must be difficult and complex . . . Poets like Auden and Spender abandoned this feminine conception of poetry and returned to the old, arrogant principle – which was Yeats's too – that it is the poet's job to make sense of the world, to simplify it, to put shape on it. The fact that these younger poets proposed to stylize their world in accordance with communist doctrine or psycho-analytical theory (both things repugnant to Yeats) is comparatively irrelevant. Whatever their system was, they stood with Yeats for system against chaos, for a positive art against a passive impressionism. Where Eliot had seen misery, frustration, and ruins, they saw heroic struggle – or, sometimes, heroic defeat – and they saw ruins rebuilding. (p. 191)

When he finally salutes Yeats as 'an example of zest', MacNeice also seems to discover in his poetry the fullblooded humanity of soul and flesh for which 'An Eclogue for Christmas' longs:

> whether it is nostalgic, love-lorn, cynical, darkly prophetic, angry over politics, or embittered over old age, there is nearly always a leaping vitality – the vitality of Cleopatra waiting for the asp. The poet kicks against life but that is because his demands from life are high. (p. 197)

While MacNeice was completing *The Poetry of W. B. Yeats* in America, he was simultaneously redefining his own aesthetic in relation to politics and war. 'The Poet in England Today: A Reassessment' (March 1940), like 'The Tower that Once', both breaks with the past and carries forward fundamental axioms into the new context: 'in the long run a poet must choose between being politically ineffectual and poetically false'. The following passage, which illuminates *Plant and Phantom*, resists the polarization of public and private poetry:

> If the artist declines to live in a merely political pigeonhole, it does not follow that he has to live in a vacuum. Man is a political animal, not a political cog. And to shun dogma does not mean to renounce belief . . . Some of the poets who renounced the Ivory Tower were ready to enter a Brazen Tower

> of political dogma; where the Ivory Tower represents isolation from men in general, the Brazen Tower represents isolation from men as individuals (witness the typical entowered politician) and also from oneself as an individual. Bad logic demanded a choice between the Towers, but salutary self-deceit allowed many of the Brazen school to leave the door open. The impact of the war with its terrible threat of genuine spiritual imprisonment has brought them again out of doors. The poet is once more to be a mouth instead of a megaphone, and poetry, one hopes, is to develop organically from the organic premisses of life – of life as it is lived, not of life when it is dried into algebra. (*SCLM*, pp. 113–14)

'Broken Windows' (see page 89) represents the next stage in MacNeice's theoretical progress.

MacNeice's arguments with Yeats and Eliot are not simply a generational quarrel: they channel his artistic quarrel with himself. By producing in evidence 'My Case-Book', itself interleaved with extracts from MacNeice's theorizing about poetry at Marlborough and Oxford, *Modern Poetry* blends the development of twentieth-century poetry with the growth of a poet's mind. Such autobiographical criticism explains, directly and indirectly, how the poet who lulled himself in sound-words and word-sounds became the poet of *Autumn Journal*. MacNeice is hard on aestheticism and pure form because that is where his own poetry originated (Pure Form had been Anthony Blunt's doctrine at Marlborough). 'Eclogue by a Five-barred Gate' dramatizes MacNeice's early dialectic between form and material, the aesthetic and the functional. This is the most authentically 'classical' of his eclogues. It takes from the *Idylls* of Theocritus and *Eclogues* of Virgil not only their dialogue format, but the situation of a stylized pastoral landscape in which shepherds discourse and engage in musical and poetic contests. MacNeice's pastoral, however, operates both as allegory and as irony. The rustic speech with which his two shepherds begin the poem proves to be just one aspect of their literary affectation, affectation which represents distance from the reality personified by the third contributor to the dialogue, Death. When Death asks for their 'credentials' the shepherds reply in an idiom which veers from the pasture to the salon:

> 1. I am a shepherd of the Theocritean breed,
> Been pasturing my songs, man and boy, this thirty year –
> 2. And for me too my pedigree acceptances
> Have multiplied beside the approved streams.

Death – a severe literary critic – rebukes them for 'dialect and . . . pedantry'. The relation of these shepherd–poets to Death prefigures that of Ryan and Craven to their mentor Grettir. In both cases the third party, absent from 'An Eclogue for Christmas', articulates MacNeice's self-critical instincts. But the critical ground shifts between 1934 and 1936. The three eclogues move from the question of a decadent civilization, to the question of poetry's social and universal responsibilities, to the question of more specifically political choices. The two shepherds more or less begin where 'A' and 'B' leave off, Ryan and Craven where the shepherds leave off. The latter tell Death at the outset that 'poets are sleepers', dedicated to aesthetic reverie: 'The sleeping beauty behind the many-coloured hedge'. When Death introduces the themes of spring and mortality, they respond with the Georgian earth-cult ('I wore canvas shoes, / Could feel the earth') and the nineties sensation-cult ('I feel a wave intensely bitter-sweet and topped with silver'). Here MacNeice satirizes his own juvenilia and parodies elements in 'An Eclogue for Christmas' ('Let the balls of my feet bounce on the turf', 'But yet there is beauty narcotic and deciduous'). Death, who believes in the poet as one who can 'quote the prices / Of significant living and decent dying', tells them: 'This escapism of yours is blasphemy.' He goads them into producing better work by asking them to recount their dreams. This tactic, on the part of MacNeice as well as Death, reflects not only his habitual belief in dreams as an inspirational source, but the Yeatsian motto 'In dreams begins responsibility.' Previously Death has quoted Yeats against the shepherds: 'All you do is burke the other and terrible beauty' ('A terrible beauty is born' – 'Easter, 1916'). The two dreams end in visions which arise out of genuine spiritual and sexual experience. We may feel that these dreams too have not discarded mannerism – 'my feet plashing in the tops of the wheat' – but then, neither has 'Birmingham'. The point is that aestheticism is trying to become functional. The eclogue's climax translates the 'pastures new' of Milton's 'Lycidas' into a landscape of inescapable destiny: not 'Thanatos in Greek' but 'the thing behind the word', which the shepherds have been dodging. The chilling sense of dissolution anticipates effects in MacNeice's later poetry:

> D. So; they are gone; life in my land . . .
> There is no life as there is no land.
> They are gone and I am alone
> With a gate the façade of a mirage.

The wartime poem 'When We Were Children', originally the 'Postscript' to *Springboard*, can be read as a comment on artistic development as well as on growing up. It indicates that a tension between 'colour' and 'meaning' persists at various levels of MacNeice's theory and practice:

> When we were children words were coloured
> (Harlot and murder were dark purple)
> And language was a prism, the light
>   A conjured inlay on the grass,
> Whose rays today are concentrated
>   And language grown a burning-glass.

His love of the prismatic makes colour, or 'twopence coloured', a recurrent metaphor for the suggestive powers of words, for the poet's technical box of tricks, for language 'with style on it' (*MP*, p. 35). *Modern Poetry* never disputes that language's quality can exceed its quantity: 'Even now words like "gold" and "roses" tend to strike me as if written in block capitals . . . A controlled flamboyance of diction has always moved me, so that I have never subscribed to the Wordsworthian exclusive crusade for home-spun' (p. 43). The stanza quoted above might sum up MacNeice's progress from the uncontrolled flamboyance of *Blind Fireworks* to the more 'concentrated' poet of conscience and responsibility. The final stanza recapitulates the challenge posed by the 1930s to the 'talents' of poets and the premisses of poetry. It admits the adult, historical necessities of content and context, of 'time and meaning'. But MacNeice also looks forward to further creative as well as personal syntheses, in which the primal aesthetic impulse will play its full part:

> Now we are older and our talents
> Accredited to time and meaning,
> To handsel joy requires a new
> Shuffle of cards behind the brain
> Where meaning shall remarry colour
> And flowers be timeless once again.

2

MacNeice always insisted that poems are made with words. 'When We Were Children' evokes a linguistic Garden of Eden (Carrickfergus rectory again) in which the spectrum of language corresponds to the spectrum of life. If, as *Modern Poetry* declares, 'the poet's first business is *mentioning* things' (p. 5) then he must be open to a variety of vocabulary as well as of phenomena. A combination of dialect and pedantry is not good enough. In his essay 'A Man of the Thirties' Geoffrey Grigson observes: 'Eliot, wrote [Wyndham] Lewis, had instilled a "*fear of speech* – a terror of the *word*". But Eliot's spell had been broken by the volubility of W. H. Auden, for whom words had no terror.' MacNeice was equally voluble – the size of his and Auden's collected works says something about the thirties generation – and their combined verbal flow swept away any linguistic decorums still guarded by Eliot and Yeats. *Autumn Journal* alone is a cornucopia of richly variegated language, not only a catalogue but a thesaurus:

> I loved her with peacock's eyes and the wares of Carthage,
> With glass and gloves and gold and a powder puff
> With blasphemy, camaraderie, and bravado
> And lots of other stuff. (I)

The poem's values too favour volubility and verbal range: the lover 'Whose words would tumble over each other and pelt / From pure excitement', the Ancient Greeks who 'talked philosophy or smut in cliques'. Lively demotic idiom criticizes narrow systems and the terminology that constructs them:

So blow the bugles over the metaphysicians,
Let the pure mind return to the Pure Mind;
I must be content to remain in the world of Appearance
And sit on the mere appearance of a behind. (XIII)

Slang, like smut, puts a brake on excessive abstraction, although MacNeice can also command philosophy's own language. An important passage in *Modern Poetry* declares urban slang, the linguistic ferment of the city, as vital a force as 'homespun':

> Popular images harden into clichés and so lose vividness, no longer call up a picture. But the popular imagination, as shown, for example, in the American wisecrack, is something with which the poet should stay in communion. Poetry can become too niggling. Synge was right when he said 'in countries where the imagination of the people, and the language they use, is rich and living, it is possible for a writer to be rich and copious in his words, and at the same time to give the reality, which is the root of all poetry, in a comprehensive and natural form', but he was wrong in implying that such language is nowadays found only among peasants. Witness the English music-halls or the newspaper articles of many of the sporting journalists, the slang talk of New York or the stories of Ring W. Lardner. (pp. 102–3)

The antidote to Pure Form and Pure Mind is 'impure poetry'. The Preface to *Modern Poetry* begins: 'This book is a plea for *impure* poetry, that is, for poetry conditioned by the poet's life and the world around him.' In the chapter on 'Obscurity' MacNeice pronounces: 'When we leave Eliot or Pound or Yeats and come to Auden or Spender, we enter a more vulgar world' (p. 169). In this world demotic idiom serves a democracy of content and attitude; the poet as Everyman displaces aristocratic and esoteric models of his role:

> My own prejudice, therefore, is in favour of poets whose worlds are not too esoteric. I would have a poet able-bodied, fond of talking, a reader of the newspapers, capable of pity and laughter, informed in economics, appreciative of women,

> involved in personal relationships, actively interested in politics, susceptible to physical impressions. (p. 198)

This is – up to a point – the poet of *Autumn Journal*, and it indicates the relation and distance between Yeats's 'unity of being' and MacNeice's 'concrete poet'. However, 'vulgarity', is not only a principle of content but a principle of form. MacNeice's 'Alphabet of Literary Prejudices', compiled ten years later, makes this clear:

> *Vulgarity*, Fear of, can be as vulgar as anything. Just as a wing three-quarter who's to score in Rugby football must generally hug the touch-line, so creative literature, which by its nature involves personal feelings, must run the risk of sentimentality. But it's better to be sometimes sentimental, over-coloured, hyperbolical or merely obvious than to play for safety always and get nowhere. Virgil, Shakespeare, Dickens and countless others were thrust into touch in their time. (*SCLM*, p. 147)

So Pure Form gives way, not to No Form, but to formal risk. *Modern Poetry* may stress 'communication', but it also stresses 'entertainment', and protects poetry's integrity as 'creation – having a new unity of its own, something in its shape which makes it poetry' (p. 30). *The Poetry of W. B. Yeats* seems anxious to correct possible imbalances in its predecessor. The Preface emphasizes that a poem does more than communicate: 'it is also a separate self; in the same way a living animal is an individual although it is on the one hand conditioned by heredity and environment and the laws of nature in general and on the other hand has a function outside itself, is a link in a chain' (p. 15). Several passages elaborate the interdependence of form and content:

> Form must not be thought of as a series of rigid moulds. All matter is to some extent *informed* to start with; and the very selection of matter is a formalistic activity. On the other hand artistic form is more than a mere method or convenience or discipline or, of course, décor . . . Artists use form not merely to express some alien matter but because form itself is a spiritual principle which calls for expression in matter. The

> relationship between form and matter is like a marriage; matter must find itself in form and form must find itself in matter. (p. 19)

In *Modern Poetry* MacNeice's approach is to demystify form and technique by projecting the poet as 'a specialist in something which everyone practises', rather than an initiate into esoteric skills:

> The poet has no greater number of muscles than the ordinary conversationalist; he merely has more highly developed muscles and better co-ordination. And he practises his activity according to a stricter set of rules . . . The absence of the spoken voice, of the face, of the particular place and time, must be compensated by a far greater precision of diction, by greater architectonic. (pp. 32–3)

The thirties poets devoted considerable architectonic effort to the renewal of traditional forms. MacNeice sees them as following Yeats in this respect. Thus the pressure of subject matter paradoxically encouraged shape. A message required a more clearcut medium than free verse could usually provide. Hence the revival of set modes – verse-epistle, ode, eclogue, ballad, song – as well as of set stanzas. Just as the purging of poeticisms left poets 'again free, if they want to, to decorate' (*MP*, p. 142), so the free-verse purge freed them back into purposeful constraints: 'in general I myself prefer the more regular kinds of verse because I think that if you are going to poise your phrases at all they will usually need more poise than can be given them by the mere arranging of them in lines . . . the poet's *matter* tends in [free verse] to appear insufficiently digested or distilled; a technical problem often helps a poet to get his own meaning clear to himself' (p. 117). The 'Alphabet of Literary Prejudices', which considers that free verse 'with rare exceptions ought to be dropped,' again defines formal colour as an instrument of meaning: 'Verse is a precision instrument and owes its precision very largely to the many and subtle differences which an ordinary word can acquire from its place in a rhythmical scheme' (*SCLM*, p. 143).

However, MacNeice's formal procedures during the 1930s did

not closely imitate Yeats's stanzaic perfection any more than they did Eliot's highly specialized irregularities. His onomatopoeic bias initially led him more to rhyme and rhythm than to overall shape. And discursive priorities compelled his forms, like Auden's, to operate more as vehicles and less as ends in themselves. The eclogues and other longer poems of the 1930s compromise in various ways between free verse, blank verse and rhyme. 'An Eclogue for Christmas' and 'Valediction', for instance, are written in unpredictable couplets. The first forty lines of 'Eclogue by a Five-barred Gate' themselves decorate 'the thing behind the word' with couplets, an ABAB pattern, rhyming on repeated words, internal rhyme and no rhyme. Conversely, MacNeice's stanzaic poems depart from norms of line length and even stanza length. 'Mayfly' reduces its five-line base to four lines, enlarges it to seven. The luxurious quatrains of 'Snow' play off longer lines against pentameter:

> The room was suddenly rich and the great bay-window was
> Spawning snow and pink roses against it . . .

He is strikingly fond of the long couplet ('Trains in the Distance', 'Evening Indoors', 'River in Spate', 'Birmingham', 'Museums', 'Nature Morte', 'Sunday Morning', 'The Glacier'). Like 'Sunday Morning', 'Spring Voices' combines long couplets with sonnet form:

> The small householder now comes out warily
> Afraid of the barrage of sun that shouts cheerily,
> Spring is massing forces, birds wink in air,
> The battlemented chestnuts volley green fire,
> The pigeons banking on the wind, the hoots of cars,
> Stir him to run wild, gamble on horses, buy cigars;
> Joy lies before him to be ladled and lapped from his hand –
> Only that behind him, in the shade of his villa, memories stand
> Breathing on his neck and muttering that all this has happened
> before,
> Keep the wind out, cast no clout, try no unwarranted jaunts
> untried before,
> But let the spring slide by nor think to board its car

For it rides West to where the tangles of scrap-iron are;
Do not walk, these voices say, between the bucking clouds alone
Or you may loiter into a suddenly howling crater, or fall, jerked
back, garrotted by the sun.

Besides variety of line length there is again variety of rhyme: trisyllabic off-rhyme (warily, cheerily), ordinary off-rhyme, the repeated word (before). Assonantal effects, including the internal rhymes 'out–clout' and 'loiter–crater', contribute to the orchestration of spring as conflicting noise. But sonnet form gives 'Spring Voices' its backbone. The division of the middle couplet, dividing the poem equally between its voices, breaks functionally with octet–sestet structure. And the final couplet makes sure of its finality in contrast with the previous six. That twenty-five syllable splurge is certainly one instance of over-coloured vulgarity, of boldly hugging the touchline.

Autumn Journal is a formal as well as a thematic culmination. Its binding verse-dynamic resolves all the organizational uncertainties of the eclogues, and all theoretical doubt as to the morality of colour in relation to meaning. Here indeed 'matter . . . finds itself in form and form . . . finds itself in matter'. MacNeice maximizes his metrical assets by adapting to extended discursive purposes a quatrain of irregular line length. The quatrain's basic rhyming modes are ABCB and ABAC. These alternate until section XII breaks the pattern. Among local variations, which can also occur within sections, are the feminine rhymes in the first twenty-eight lines of section XII, and the ABCA/ABBC modes of XXIII ('The road ran downhill into Spain'). The latter intensify an essential virtue of the quatrain: its potential for either closure or openness. Section XXIII ends with the unrhymed last word allowing the accusing cock-crow to hang in the air:

Whereas these people contain truth, whatever
Their nominal façade.
Listen: a whirr, a challenge, an aubade –
It is the cock crowing in Barcelona.

Switches of mode help to negotiate significant transitions between sections. Thus in section VIII the ABAC mode accompanies the dying fall of Munich:

Glory to God for Munich.
And stocks go up and wrecks
Are salved and politicans' reputations
Go up like Jack-on-the-Beanstalk; only the Czechs
Go down and without fighting.

Immediately afterwards the ironic tone of section IX is initiated by the capacity of the ABCB mode for more emphatic closure, for epigram. Metrical evenness satirizes the resumption of 'even tenor':

Now we are back to normal, now the mind is
Back to the even tenor of the usual day
Skidding no longer across the uneasy camber
Of the nightmare way.

On a larger scale, MacNeice can choose whether to stress the self-contained character of the quatrain, or to suppress some of its identity within a larger momentum. Sometimes refrain adds a further binding factor. Section XXIV, which recapitulates all the quatrain's modes, also unifies them with its lullaby. At the climax ABCB alternates with the more dispersed rhyme scheme ABCA. This helps to produce the larger formal compromise between openness and closure:

Tonight we sleep
On the banks of Rubicon – the die is cast;
There will be time to audit
The accounts later, there will be sunlight later
And the equation will come out at last.

The protean quatrain of *Autumn Journal* accommodates every change of tone and angle. It is a precision instrument for establishing all the poem's other alternations: between pictures and generalizations, optimism and irony, necessity and possibility, historical flux and artistic poise.

Ten years, 1938–48, separate *The Earth Compels* and *Holes in the Sky*. These collections contain poems which fulfil aspects of MacNeice's earlier aesthetic. Among poems already discussed, 'Carrickfergus' and 'Bagpipe Music' indicate the formal importance of sounds. The former takes its cue not from a set quatrain, but from the 'informing' of that quatrain by the noises and voices of childhood. 'Bagpipe Music' finds yet another rhythm for the long couplet (already imitative of a river and traffic movements) including some particularly 'vulgar' feminine rhymes: 'Blavatsky–taxi'. Two love poems, 'The Sunlight on the Garden' and the central section of 'Trilogy for X', discipline internal rhyme into a dramatically pointed punctuation. In the former the feminine rhyme which ends/begins successive lines rhetorically stylizes the compulsion of historical and natural processes: 'The earth compels, upon it / Sonnets and birds descend . . .' Section II is the masterpiece of 'Trilogy for X'. All its sound-patterns are relevant to a tension between post-coital quiet and the outer world epitomized by intrusive noise:

> And love hung still as crystal over the bed
>   And filled the corners of the enormous room;
> The boom of dawn that left her sleeping, showing
>   The flowers mirrored in the mahogany table.
>
> O my love, if only I were able
>   To protract this hour of quiet after passion,
> Not ration happiness but keep this door for ever
>   Closed on the world, its own world closed within it.

MacNeice's internal rhyme and assonance have never functioned so delicately as in 'still–crystal–filled' which suggests silence by evoking a chandelier that might be shattered. To add to the complexity, the last line of one quatrain rhymes with the first of the next. This, in conjunction with the internal rhyming, parallels the gravitational pull of 'The Sunlight on the Garden'. A rhythmic undertow echoes the inevitable progress whereby 'dawn's waves trouble with the bubbling minute'. However, the poem ends with a full rhyme and a couplet which subliminally continue to assert 'our one night's identity':

> The first train passes and the windows groan,
>   Voices will hector and your voice become
> A drum in tune with theirs, which all last night
>   Like sap that fingered through a hungry tree
> Asserted our one night's identity.

Perhaps because time and permanence matter so much, and hence flux and pattern, MacNeice's love poetry draws on his deepest formal inspiration. 'Meeting Point' (from *Plant and Phantom*) brilliantly combines stanza and syntax into a formal unit which reproduces love's suspension of temporal laws:

> Time was away and she was here
> And life no longer what it was,
> The bell was silent in the air
> And all the room one glow because
> Time was away and she was here.

While austerities remain or take new forms as in the Achill sequence (see page 32), *Holes in the Sky* restores pre-war richness to some of MacNeice's structures. Freewheeling on all fronts, 'The Cyclist' explicitly delights in a liberation of metre, metaphor, rhythm, syntax:

> And reaching the valley the boy must pedal again
> Left-right-left but meanwhile
> For ten seconds more can move as the horse in the chalk
> Moves unbeginningly calmly
> Calmly regardless of tenses and final clauses
> Calmly unendingly moves.

The three poems that follow 'The Cyclist' – 'Woods', 'Elegy for Minor Poets' and 'Autolycus' – share a six-line stanza, a closely woven verbal texture, and subtextual comment on MacNeice's aesthetic. The poems are less remarkable for what they do with the stanza itself, than for the mature manner in which MacNeice handles the relations between imagery and statement, form and informality. The conclusion of 'Woods' makes its point about English culture by means of sensuous realization and a deceptive syntactical 'inconsequence':

> And always we walk out again. The patch
> Of sky at the end of the path grows and discloses
> An ordered open air long ruled by dyke and fence,
> With geese whose form and gait proclaim their consequence,
> Pargetted outposts, windows browed with thatch,
> And cow pats – and inconsequent wild roses.

In 'Woods', and more obliquely in the other two poems, landscape functions as the terrain of MacNeice's imagination. Walking out of English woods balances their ultimate 'tameness' against what bog, rock and 'the wilds of Mayo' (wilder than the roses) represent. The minor poets run an allegorical obstacle-course between 'Promised Land' and 'dark bogs'. The poem's speaker does not detach himself from the ordeal of these martyrs to the mysteries of the creative process:

> Let the sun clamber on to the notebook, shine,
> And fill in what they groped for between each line.

In celebrating Autolycus, the 'master pedlar' from *The Winter's Tale*, MacNeice evidently identifies his own tensions with 'A gay world . . . pocked and scored / With childish horrors'. If 'Woods' reflects on divided cultural affiliation and iconography, 'Elegy for Minor Poets' on the chanciness of inspiration, then 'Autolycus' marvels at the Shakespearian 'mastery' that can resolve all dialectics, dialects and gropings:

> Eclectic always, now extravagant,
> Sighting his matter through a timeless prism
> He ranged his classical bric-à-brac in grottos
> Where knights of Ancient Greece had Latin mottoes
> And fishermen their flapjacks – none should want
> Colour for lack of an anachronism.

Terence Brown comments: 'the hotch-potch of diction in "Autolycus" seems to capture the mixture of styles and forms which makes Shakespeare's last plays so enchanting' (*Sceptical Vision*). Thus MacNeice's own eclectic extravagance backs up one of his basic critical themes: the necessary impurity which makes poetry a compound of talking 'crystal' and 'gabbing earth'. 'Autolycus' also implies that vulgar colour cannot go too far. As poems about MacNeice's aesthetic, however, these speculate as well as consummate. On the positive side, they contain signposts to the future. 'Woods' is concerned with the stuff of myth, preferably beyond the reach of social ordering, and its reference to *Morte d'Arthur* portends the symbolic questing of MacNeice's later poetry. The appeal of Shakespeare's romances also underlines the growing attraction of fantasy and myth now that chunks of life are wearing thin. At the same time, the perfectly phrased 'Elegy' is ominously conscious of poets 'Who knew all the words but failed to achieve the Word'.

MacNeice did suffer from an attack of wordiness in the late 1940s and early 1950s. If during the war years 'I myself grew more relaxed while my poetry tightened up' (sleeve note to Argo reading of his poems), the reverse now seemed to be the case. In 'The Stygian Banks' and 'Letter from India' (from *Holes in the Sky*), in 'The North Sea', 'Mahabalipuram' and 'The Window' which he added to his *Collected Poems 1925–1948*, and throughout *Ten Burnt Offerings* (1952), the thirties verbal mill goes on loosely grinding without its grist. MacNeice flounders between travelogue and metaphysics and efforts to unite the two. The fusion of *Autumn Journal* has become fission. Visits to India and Pakistan (1947) and a year and a half in Greece (1950–1) sparked off mistaken attempts to reconstitute thirties reportage in new terms:

> Here where the banyan weeps her children,
> Where pavements flower with wounds and fins
> And kite and vulture hold their vigil
> Which never ends, never begins
> To end, this world which spins and grins
> Seems a mere sabbath of bacilli . . .

Although MacNeice was deeply moved by the turmoil of the subcontinent, little personal and social urgency charges these sense impressions and the concluding speculation. The purely speculative 'Stygian Banks' ends:

> Glory is what?
> We cannot answer in words though every verb is a hint of it
> And even Die is a live word. Nor can we answer
> In any particular action for each is adulterate coin
> However much we may buy with it. No answer
> Is ours – yet we are unique
> In putting the question at all and a false coin
> Presumes a true mint somewhere. Your child's hoop,
> Though far from a perfect circle, holds the road

And the road is far from straight, yet like a bee
Can pollinate the towns for the towns though ugly
Have blossom in them somewhere. Far from perfect
Presumes perfection *where*? A catechism the drums
Asseverate day-long, night-long: Glory is what?
A question! . . . Now it is Spring.

This betrays its own desperation as abstraction in pursuit of image, image in pursuit of point, humanism in pursuit of validation, technique in pursuit of inspiration, colour in pursuit of meaning. The best insight, 'a false coin / Presumes a true mint somewhere', might be an insight into the writing itself. Throughout 'The Stygian Banks' the true mint of MacNeice's ideas, symbols and images (glory, doubt, spring, blossom, drums) can be discerned behind the counterfeit. Similarly, 'Our Sister Water' ponderously abstracts one of MacNeice's most specific archetypes, and 'Day of Renewal' manages to make his autobiography uninteresting. The few alive passages in this whole phase, such as the opening of 'Day of Renewal', tend to acknowledge some aesthetic predicament. 'The Window' addresses MacNeice's familiar antinomy of flux and pattern in an over-exclamatory manner: 'How, yes how! To achieve in a world of flux and bonfires / Something of art's coherence . . . ?' However, it concludes with a beautiful epiphany which imagines fresh inspiration and integration:

Those are friends who once were foreign
  And gently shines the face of doom,
The pot of flowers inspires the window,
The air blows in, the vistas open
  And a sweet scent pervades the room.

'The Window' suggests that MacNeice, in keeping with his previous aesthetic, is looking to life for a coherence which in turn will give coherence to his art. This may explain why, having attempted in separation some of the methods that *Autumn Journal* fused, he tried to recapture the old magic by writing a sequel. *Autumn Sequel* is 'similarly hinged to the autumn of 1953' (Prefatory note). With the exception of a few passages, *Autumn Sequel* proves that, artistically speaking, you can never go back. It also proves that a long poem needs an animating formal principle rather than a hinge. MacNeice does not succeed in creating a dynamic which derives from either psychic or cultural pressures. *Terza rima* (pentameter triplets ABA, BCB, etc.) is a notoriously difficult scheme in English, and it specifically rules out the rhythmical and tonal relations that construct the dramatic poise of *Autumn Journal*. It may be a metre for narrative and flux, but not for argument and climax. *Autumn Sequel* hangs metaphysics and travelogue (within Britain) on autobiography which now emphasizes friendship. MacNeice's Utopian affections fail to recreate the lyric drama of *Autumn Journal*, perhaps because the tension between lonely centre and populated circumference has slackened. *Autumn Sequel* tends to be nostalgic for the forces which shaped both its prototype and the wartime poetry. But if MacNeice cannot make alternations of work and holiday as immediate as alternations of peace and war, this is the fault not of subject matter but of form repeated as formula. A gambit like 'To work – To Beaconsfield' or 'So this is Glastonbury' is doubly an anti-climax when one senses the sub-Autumn-Journalese. While would-be simplicity falls flat, would-be colour is hectically over-applied. The conceits and colloquialisms cover banality with a jerky vivacity:

> And now it is August, fading what was green,
> Forgetting what was death, jogging along,
> Two plain, two purl, to end the Augustan scene
>
> More sock than buskin, more cheap wine than song.
> Shortly we must turn over an old leaf
> To prove the year goes round while we go wrong.

In default of true informing energy, the phrases seem separate units within a static frame.

The main exception to a pervasive divorce between colour and meaning is the portrayal of Dylan Thomas (cantos II, XVIII, and XX). It may be significant that MacNeice relishes 'Gwilym' as a 'maker', an Autolycus, a verbal fantasist: 'A whole masque / Of tones and cadences – the organ boom, / The mimicry, then the chuckles'. Also, Thomas's death heightens the poem's sense of life and draws on MacNeice's powers of elegy:

> Since, even if an afterlife were true,
> Gwilym without his body, his booming voice,
> Would simply not be Gwilym . . .

But despite such intensifications, and the emergence of motifs he treats more successfully later on, *Autumn Sequel* remains largely self-paraphrase or self-parody: a translation of MacNeice's poetry into less than his prose. It confirms that the era of 'volubility' is over.

3

'After *The Earth Compels* I tired of tourism and after *Autumn Journal* I tired of journalism,' says MacNeice in 'Experiences with Images' (*SCLM*, p. 161). As we have seen, this fatigue unfortunately wore off. However, MacNeice's wartime changes of theory and practice eventually paid still richer dividends in the poems of *Solstices* (1961, section XIII of the *Collected Poems*) and *The Burning Perch* (1963, XIV). *Visitations* (1957, XII) contains a number of forerunners.

MacNeice's post-war criticism detected hiatus in the literary sphere too: 'The only improvement I can see . . . is a negative one: we have purged ourselves of some nonsense.' This comes from an article on 'The English Literary Scene Today' (1947), which nevertheless spots some positive trends: away from chunks of life, and towards 'metaphysical meaning', religious consciousness 'in the widest sense', and rediscovery of 'the half-forgotten axiom that poetry is not just a matter of externals or of rational content'. MacNeice is evidently talking about his own preoccupations. As a writer for radio, released from documentary and propaganda, he was now exploring the artistic possibilities of folk-tales, myths, and 'satirical fantasy' (as he termed his *March Hare Saga*, 1945–6). Everyone agrees that *The Dark Tower*, broadcast in January 1946, is MacNeice's best radio play. However, like all his dramatic output, it has the essentially subsidiary importance MacNeice attached to Yeats's plays: 'his exercise in this genre undoubtedly had valuable effects upon his lyric' (*PWBY*, p. 170). *The Dark Tower* is a quest-allegory, influenced by Malory's knights and immediately suggested by Robert Browning's poem

'Childe Roland to the Dark Tower came'. MacNeice's Introductory Note to the published text (1947) explains why he subtitled *The Dark Tower* 'a radio parable play'. Disowning 'realism' still more emphatically than in earlier statements, he outlines some ideas which underlie the poems of a decade later:

> My own impression is that pure 'realism' is in our time almost played out, though most works of fiction of course will remain realistic *on the surface*. The single-track mind and the single-plane novel or play are almost bound to falsify the world in which we live. The fact that there is method in madness and the fact that there is fact in fantasy (and equally fantasy in 'fact') have been brought home to us not only by Freud and other psychologists but by events themselves. This being so, reportage can no longer masquerade as art. So the novelist, abandoning the 'straight' method of photography, is likely to resort once more not only to the twist of plot but to all kinds of other twists which may help him to do justice to the world's complexity. Some element of parable therefore, far from making a work thinner and more abstract, ought to make it more concrete. Man does after all live by symbols. (p. 21)

In *Varieties of Parable*, which comprises the Clark Lectures he gave at Cambridge in 1963, MacNeice discusses much more fully the significance of 'parable' for the time and implicitly for his own aesthetic. The discussion covers Samuel Beckett, Harold Pinter and William Golding (new writers to whom he obviously feels akin) as well as old parable-favourites like *Everyman*, *The Faerie Queene*, *Pilgrim's Progress*, the *Alice* books, Kafka's *The Trial* and *The Castle*, and the fantasy tales of George MacDonald. He initially defines parable in terms which recall the Introductory Note to *The Dark Tower* and are relevant to *Solstices* and *The Burning Perch*. Having approved the *OED* definition, 'any saying or narration in which something is expressed in terms of something else . . . any kind of enigmatical or dark saying', he adds: 'a kind of double-level writing, or, if you prefer it, sleight of hand' (pp. 2–3). However, the complete practical adaptation of parable to poetry, or of poetry to parable, was a gradual process. On the one hand, MacNeice had always written parable in some shape or form ('River in Spate' and 'Chess', for instance, would qualify under the above definitions); on the other, after the war technical progress lagged behind theory. Thus 'Experiences with Images' (1949), while assimilating wartime developments, to some extent conceives in prospect what *Varieties of Parable* interprets in retrospect:

> since *Autumn Journal* I have been eschewing the news-reel and attempting a stricter kind of drama which largely depends upon structure. On analysis (though I have never thought of it this way when in the act of writing) this structural tightening-up seems to involve four things: (1) the selection of – or perhaps the being selected by – a single theme which itself is a strong symbol, (2) a rhythmical pattern which holds that theme together, (3) syntax (a more careful ordering of sentences, especially in relation to the verse pattern), and (4) a more structural use of imagery. (*SCLM*, pp. 161–2)

MacNeice goes on to distinguish a poem like 'Snow' in which the images are 'bang centre stage' from 'The Springboard' which

> though rational in its working out, begins with two irrational premisses – the dream picture of a naked man standing on a springboard in the middle of the air over London and the irrational assumption that it is his duty to throw himself down from there as a sort of ritual sacrifice. This will be lost on those who have no dream logic, as will other poems of mine such as 'The Dowser' and 'Order to View' which are a blend of rational allegory and dream suggestiveness. (p. 163)

All MacNeice's parables probably belong to some point on the curve from 'rational allegory' to 'dream suggestiveness', with the latter quality most densely clustered in *The Burning Perch*. 'Convoy' might illustrate allegory at its most rational, as strongly ruled parallels: 'This is a bit like us . . .' 'Figure of Eight' (*Visitations*) and 'Charon' (*The Burning Perch*) contrast as versions of the journey of life. The former is rational allegory which ends suggestively:

But, winding up the black thread of his days,
The wheels roll on and make it all too plain
Who will be there to meet him at the station.

The latter is more four-dimensionally mysterious throughout, and its 'dream logic' culminates in a full nightmare incarnation:

We flicked the flashlight
And there was the ferryman just as Virgil
And Dante had seen him. He looked at us coldly
And his eyes were dead and his hands on the oar
Were black with obols and varicose veins
Marbled his calves and he said to us coldly:
If you want to die you will have to pay for it.

Section 2 of the next chapter will consider how the structures and strategies of parable articulate MacNeice's concern with the question of belief, with the challenges to humanistic optimism which Charon's 'dark saying' – a parable within a parable – sums up. However, doing justice to 'the world's complexity' depended on remaking the fundamentals of poetic technique. It is notable that MacNeice did not revert to Eliot's 'feminine' aesthetic when confronted afresh by existential complexity. Instead, he exerted greater pressure on form, pushing forward its frontiers in several directions. Broadly speaking, these might be listed as: firstly, the relating of 'a more structural use of imagery' to 'a strong symbol'; secondly, the parallel reciprocity between a more structural use of syntax and a unifying 'rhythmical pattern'; and thirdly, a more structural role too for the intrinsic qualities of words and idioms themselves. In all three cases MacNeice sharpens poetry as a precision instrument, and deepens the bonding between colour and meaning.

Written in 1940, 'Order to View', which MacNeice singles out in 'Experiences with Images', anticipates the technical procedures of later parables:

It was a big house, bleak;
Grass on the drive;
We had been there before
But memory, weak in front of

A blistered door, could find
Nothing alive now;
The shrubbery dripped, a crypt
Of leafmould dreams; a tarnished
Arrow over an empty stable
Shifted a little in the tenuous wind . . .

The strong symbol of the house is crucial to this interweaving of folk-tale and fairy-tale ingredients, archetypal and psychic connotations, dream logic. The house draws together familiar images like the 'leaf-mould' of 'Happy Families' and a contrastingly hopeful 'one wish, / A rainbow bubble'. The bubble blends abstract and concrete as do other aspects of this semi-tangible scene, which expresses in a new way MacNeice's obsession with petrifaction and stasis. The 'deadly illness', like the house, seems multi-level. It might be personal neurosis, it might be 'derelict England' as Robyn Marsack suggests in *The Cave of Making*. In any case the effect meets MacNeice's condition that parable should be unparaphrasable. 'Reflections' (*Solstices*) is a different kind of parable. It makes everyday experience emblematic – one of the achievements for which MacNeice admired George Herbert. But 'Reflections' is again unified by a strong symbol:

The mirror above my fireplace reflects the reflected
Room in my window; I look in the mirror at night
And see two rooms, the first where left is right
And the second, beyond the reflected window, corrected
But there I am standing back to my back. The standard
Lamp comes thrice in my mirror, twice in my window,
The fire in the mirror lies two rooms away through the window,
The fire in the window lies one room away down the terrace,
My actual room stands sandwiched between confections
Of night and lights and glass . . .

This concentrates the allusions to windows and mirrors that abound in MacNeice's poetry. Terence Brown comments: 'In many poems we find a man, or the poet, peering out at events and objects through a window, conscious of the intervening glass – of separation, division, of the dualism between the perceiver and the thing perceived' (*Sceptical Vision*). In *Modern Poetry* MacNeice interprets his earlier use of mirrors in 'Perseus':

> I am describing a mood of terror when everything seems to be unreal, petrified – hence the Gorgon's head, which dominates this poem. Such a mood being especially common among children, 'the end room' implies a child's fear of long corridors. In such a mood, both when a child and when grown-up, I remember looking in mirrors and (a) thinking that my own face looked like a strange face, especially in the eyes, and (b) being fascinated and alarmed by the mysterious gleams of light *glancing* off the mirror. And, lastly, a mirror is a symbol of nihilism via solipsism. (p. 175)

However, the Gorgon's head does not dominate 'Perseus' as 'confections /Of night and lights and glass' dominate 'Reflections'. Nor does it combine petrifaction images and mirror images into as rigorous a whole. It is the difference between associative imagery and the parabolic elaboration of a primary symbol. A sense of 'through the looking-glass', governs the mutations of fire, lamp, bookcase and taxi. By presenting the self dislocated and stranded within the hall of its own mirrors, MacNeice intensively symbolizes rather than discursively expounds 'nihilism via solipsism':

> and in both directions
> I can see beyond and through the reflections the street lamps
> At home outdoors where my indoors rooms lie stranded,
> Where a taxi perhaps will drive in through the bookcase
> Whose books are not for reading and past the fire
> Which gives no warmth and pull up by my desk
> At which I cannot write since I am not lefthanded.

Structural symbolism also works on a larger scale. It may be significant that Ireland sparked off MacNeice's first *sequences* of parable poems. The Achill series in *Holes in the Sky* led to 'A Hand of Snapshots' in *Visitations* (see pages 32–3). *Solstices* follows up these prototypes with five sequences: 'Dark Age Glosses', 'Indoor Sports', 'Nature Notes', 'Sleeping Winds' and four poems centred on 'The Park'. Three of these, indeed, incorporate Irish materials: 'on the Four Masters' from 'Dark Age Glosses' features Brian Boru, 'Nature Notes' returns to childhood experiences with images, and the West wind fills St Brendan's sails: 'The long-lost ship / Flew home and into legend like a bird.' Radio plays also make a contribution: *They Met on Good Friday* (1959) which concerns the death-in-victory of Brian Boru at the Battle of Clontarf; dramatizations of Icelandic saga (1947); and *East of the Sun and West of the Moon* (1959), based on a Norwegian folk-tale, which personifies the Four Winds. More radically than 'The Closing Album' or 'Novelettes', MacNeice's later sequences put into technical practice a belief he had held since the 1930s:

> The short poem has naturally a unique concentration; even so I notice that, in spite of the popular assumption that any one 'lyric' should be entirely self-supporting, yet our appreciation of it is greatly helped by a reading of other lyrics by the same author; more than this, we think of it (generally half-consciously) as a part of a whole, constituted by its author's other poetry and often (if we are not to cant) by certain aspects of the author himself. (*SCLM*, pp. 41–2)

The sudden intensification of the sequence habit in *Solstices* underlines the generally greater mutual support between poems in the last two books. MacNeice found *Solstices* 'mostly to be scored for the same set of instruments' (*SCLM*, p. 224). Parable added to his dramatic lyric not only new masks, but also new techniques for orchestrating individual poems as facets of a larger whole.

The sequences in *Solstices* involve different kinds of unity and different kinds of parabolic method. They also sometimes comment on their own pioneering techniques. The unity of 'Dark Age Glosses' depends on comparisons between the present and the legendary past, comparisons which give the sequence a mythic resonance. For instance, the first poem, 'on the Venerable Bede', links the poem's reader to his ancestors by imagining how a parable was received by its original Anglo-Saxon audience:

> The great wooden hall with long fires down the centre,
> Their feet in the rushes, their hands tearing the meat.
> Suddenly high above them they notice a swallow enter

From the black storm and zigzag over their heads,
Then out once more into the unknown night;
And that, someone remarks, is the life of man.

'Dark Age Glosses' conjures up the so-called 'dark ages' of England, Iceland and Ireland in order to expose what is in fact dark to modern man. ('As in Their Time' in *The Burning Perch* made a similar point by more elliptical means.) MacNeice's irony probably extends to the word 'Glosses' as well. 'Gloss' can mean an explanation, a deceptive appearance, or a surface shine. If these parable poems themselves are glosses, MacNeice implies that their explanation of the world may not be wholly clear-cut. Archetypal questions, which puzzle Bede's feasters as they react to the parable of the swallow, remain puzzling: 'They close their eyes that smart from the woodsmoke: how / Can anyone even guess his whence and whither?' Although MacNeice's glosses take the shine off nostalgia for golden ages (Brian Boru's 'eighty years . . . Soured him with power and rusted him with blood'), they call attention to lost heroic and spiritual consciousness. 'On the Grettir Saga' brings back the protagonist of 'Eclogue from Iceland'. Grettir is no longer predominantly conceived as an exemplar of positive action, but unlike his twentieth-century counterpart he at least understands the significance of his fate:

But, unlike the major, Grettir was cursed,
Haunted by eyes in the dark, on his desolate
Rock on the fringe of the Arctic knew
The fear no man had ever induced in him,
And thus awaited his doom. Whereas
The major, who also was doomed, slept sound
And was merely cursed by the curse of his time.

Even the savagely ironic death of Gunnar has launched 'one great saga casting from those dark / Ages a lighthouse ray'.

'Nature Notes' is not just a series of natural images, but a set of emblems which correlate human behaviour and the natural world. This correlation produces optimistic results. 'Dandelions', 'Cats', 'Corncrakes' and 'The Sea', all introduced by the adjective 'Incorrigible' (a tougher version of 'inconsequent'), exemplify qualities and forces unamenable to the rules so distrusted by

MacNeice's poetry. What is uncontrollable in Nature at least reassures man that a similar spirit lurks in him. The sequence is stylized in a way which emphasizes a concept that underlies parable and symbolism: similitude, simile. Each phenomenon is said to be both unlike and like another (thus the unities of 'Nature Notes' preserve the principle of 'variousness'):

The Sea

Incorrigible, ruthless,
It rattled the shingly beach of my childhood,
Subtle, the opposite of earth,
And, unlike earth, capable
Any time at all of proclaiming eternity
Like something or someone to whom
We have to surrender, finding
Through that surrender life.

The last three lines of the poems invert the usual notion of a simile by making the more abstract component illustrate the more concrete. 'Indoor Sports' is inspired by the game of life and love: part strong symbol, part 'rational allegory'. This sequence again incorporates self-commentary in that the combination of 'luck' and 'skill', required both by games and by personal relations, might apply to the poems' own 'sleight-of-hand'. The final poem 'Crossword Puzzles' – an appropriate title for all MacNeice's parables – suggests how the riddles of parable challenge us: 'It is time / We left these puzzles and started to be ourselves / And started to live, is it not?' (This puzzle's answer, if it has one, might be 'I' and 'life'.) 'Sleeping Winds' leaves rational allegory for more enigmatic symbolism:

South

The wind had hidden his head in a pit in the sand
Of an uncrossable desert; something slid
Into his lack of ear, he gradually uncurled
Like a king cobra, rose and spread his hood
And swayed in time with what the charmer piped,
In time with Time, to wreck or bless the world.

The winds (bracing North, East craving for water, legendary West, charmed South) may represent latent meanings sought by humanity and accessible to parable. These poems hint at different philosophies, religions, points of the metaphysical compass.

The 'Park' sequence (not headlined as such) differs from the others in that it turns MacNeice's everyday world into a parable scenario unified by his strongest symbol so far. It also illustrates how syntax co-operates with symbol and imagery to produce such a scenario. This new look at an old poetic haunt, Regent's Park, capitalizes on the presence of the zoo. The 'Urban enclave of lawns and water' is a microcosm of corrigible Nature, of contracted human, animal, vegetable and mineral worlds:

> Fossils of flesh, fossils of stucco:
> Between them the carefully labelled flower beds
> And the litter baskets . . .
>
> ('The Park')

Human beings get the worst of these worlds. In 'The Lake in the Park' the solitary 'small clerk', descendant of the 'small householder', is mocked by 'bosomy / Trees' and courting pigeons. The juxtaposition of tame and wild animals raises questions for the former, but more seriously for man. In 'Dogs in the Park' the dogs who 'scavenge at the mouths of Stone Age caves' and then return to heel reflect their owners' leashes:

> And then they leave the park, the leads are snapped
> On to the spiky collars, the tails wag
> For no known reason and the ears are pricked
> To search through legendary copse and crag
> For legendary creatures doomed to die
> Even as they, the dogs, were doomed to live.

Various 'Stone Age echoes' in the sequence satirize the diminished condition of 'civilized' man, who may similarly have betrayed his 'legendary' ancestors (compare 'on the Grettir Saga'). The inclusiveness of the park as a symbolic location signals how parable will span the social and spiritual wings of MacNeice's poetry. The poems suggest a comprehensively doomed species, while leaving a little symbolic room for escape from the cages determined by society or a broader destiny. The stanza quoted above from 'The Park' continues:

> but also between them
> Through a grille gaily men as music
> Forcing the spring to loose the lid,
> To break the bars, to find the world.

The importance of the word 'between' in these lines recalls its role in 'Snow' and suggests again its crucial ambiguity in MacNeice's metaphysic. Does it separate or join? However, 'between' now participates in a more pervasively unusual syntax. 'The Park', which (like 'Nature Notes') rations main verbs, begins: 'Through a glass greenly men as trees walking . . .' In a review (1963) of a book about Robert Frost MacNeice says:

> I have often been surprised that reviewers of verse pay so little attention to syntax. A sentence in prose is struck forward like a golf ball; a sentence in verse can be treated like a ball in a squash court. Frost, as Brower brings out, is a master of angles . . . (*SCLM*, p. 245)

'Sunday in the Park' is the most revolutionary poem in the sequence because it most completely exploits squash-court syntax, and indicates MacNeice's increasing mastery of angles:

> No sunlight ever. Bleak trees whisper ironies,
> Carolina duck and Canada goose forget
> Their world across the water, red geraniums
> Enhance the chill, dark glasses mirror ironies,
> The prams are big with doom, the walkers-out forget
> Why they are out, London is lost, geraniums
> Stick it out in the wind, old men feel lost
> But stick it out . . .

This structure is dominated by asyndeton, i.e. the omission of conjunctions. If 'conjunction' is the paramount formal feature of *Autumn Journal*, asyndeton comes into its own in the later poetry. Its staccato effect, especially where applied to a succession of brief statements, reproduces the negative side of 'between'. It suggests that there are black holes rather than cosmic links between phenomena. The lack of logical momentum from one statement to another creates the sense that the people, flora and fauna are trapped within a directionless universe. It further 'enhances the chill' that the recurrence of certain words – ironies, forget, out, lost – conveys circularity or a dead end rather than advance: 'the walkers-out forget / Why they are out'. As for the relation between syntax and verse-pattern, it is difficult to say whether the repetitions of word and phrase-construction constitute a kind of rhyme or a kind of refrain. They certainly build up a rhythm which depends neither on stanza (although hidden quatrains play a part) nor on complete freedom of movement. The poem's musical shape is primarily determined by its syntax.

Autumn Journal represented a culmination of MacNeice's skill in adapting the period, the sentence with multiple clauses, to a metrical flow. This rationally interconnected sentence is a component, as well as a cement, of the poem's high humanism. Asyndeton, although a legitimate device, breaks the chain of the period and seems allied to some of the jumps of 'dream logic'. Like 'Sunday in the Park', 'Hold-up', 'Another Cold May' and the pioneering 'Order to View' exploit asyndeton as an ultimate means of imitating stasis or petrifaction. However, *Solstices* also contains poems which elasticate rather than frustrate the period. The interplay of shorter and longer units is anticipated in MacNeice's enthusiasm (1946) for the prose style of Apuleius, an eclectic and extravagant writer from the Latin Silver Age: 'His sentences are often as long as Cicero's but they are not "periods"; the Chinese boxes of subordinate clauses, the geometrical architectonic, have gone; in their place is an arithmetical or cumulative technique, a succession of fairly short phrases, roughly equal in length and often rhyming, often without conjunctions, just adding up and adding up' (*SCLM*, p. 131). 'Reflections' syntactically enacts its meaning by setting mirror-image clauses more and more elaborately on the march. Here repetition imitates not stasis, but the changing slots to which relativistic perception assigns phenomena: 'The fire in the mirror . . . / The fire in the window'. 'Variation on Heraclitus' employs a differently constructed long sentence which brings MacNeice's preoccupation with flux to a logical conclusion, both from a formal and thematic point of view:

> Even the walls are flowing, even the ceiling,
> Nor only in terms of physics; the pictures
> Bob on each picture rail like floats on a line
> While the books on the shelves keep reeling
> Their titles out into space and the carpet
> Keeps flying away to Arabia nor can this be where I stood –
> Where I shot the rapids I mean – when I signed
> On a line that rippled away with a pen that melted . . .

The clauses reel out in a manner which mimics the impossibility of systems keeping up with the flow of life: 'And, all you advisers on this by the time it is that, / I just do not want your advice.' The end of the poem adapts the central dictum of Heraclitus, the Greek philosopher of flux: 'You cannot step twice into the same river' – a dictum also central to MacNeice's philosophizing. 'Variation on Heraclitus' is also a variation on 'Mayfly' and 'The Individualist Speaks'. The syntax shaping the poem's form helps to establish a new angle on how the positives of flux might outweigh the negatives, on how the self might escape into its own Becoming:

> Nor need you be troubled to pin me down in my room
> Since the room and I will escape for I tell you flat:
> One cannot live in the same room twice.

The 'standard lamp' featured in 'Reflections' and 'Variation on Heraclitus' has an ironic status, since the poems query fixed perceptions, a steady-state universe and standard English. However, the latter poem shows that non-standard syntax can serve affirmation as well as irony or 'nihilism via solipsism'. This applies to its uses in MacNeice's later love poetry. 'All Over Again' takes love's timeless moment to a more technically radical extreme than 'Meeting Point'. Mostly composed of 'as if' clauses, it turns the 'forgotten sentence' of 'The Cyclist' into a structure rather than a theme. As these clauses swell out, we are seduced into accepting the conditional as the truly indicative. The end of the poem comes up with one answer to the problem of 'between'. It postulates the lovers' ecstasy as not merely an interlude but the dominant reality: 'as if / This one Between were All and we in love for years'. Suspension of the laws of time is dramatized by virtual suspension of that rule of grammar which requires a main statement. Similarly, 'Déjà Vu' (*The Burning Perch*) urges that 'Our love must extend beyond time' by consisting of a sentence which returns to its starting-point and remains in perpetual motion. 'Reflections', 'Variation on Heraclitus', 'All Over Again' and 'Déjà Vu' all make formal use of end-rhyme and special rhythms, but syntax has again been the prime mover. Overall, it has opened up for MacNeice new ways of conceiving the syntax of experience itself: its stasis or flow, its connections or hiatuses, its angles, sequences and *non sequiturs*.

MacNeice's innovative poems are marginally preoccupied with their own innovation: 'Of which to speak requires new fires of the tongue' ('All Over Again'). These fires are lit by diction as well as by syntax. 'All Over Again' unfolds the implications of its title and of 'as if'. 'Reflections' also puns on its title. 'Sunday in the Park' brings out the chill in certain words and idioms too. 'Stick it out' carries less conviction with repetition, and mutates into 'Get stuck'. 'The prams are big with doom' involves verbal and consequently other mutations. Two poems in *Solstices*, 'Icebergs' and 'Idle Talk' (see below), comment on what is happening to MacNeice's 'whole delightful world of cliché and refrain'. This phrase as used in 'Homage to Clichés' (1935) is a linguistic metaphor for our addiction to habit, to 'the automatic, the reflex'. 'Homage' partly indulges the addiction, partly probes the fears that underlie it:

> What will you have, my dear? The same again?
> . . .
> I have shut the little window that looks up the road
> Towards the tombs of the kings . . .

'Icebergs' treats the same theme more intensely and emblematically by imagining a wordless realm lurking beneath the linguistic surfaces to which we cling:

> There are no words below the water,
> Let alone phrases, let alone
> Sentences – except the one
> Sentence that tells you life is done . . .

'Homage to Clichés', like many of MacNeice's poems in the 1930s and 1940s, injects irony into its own use of cliché: it cannot always be 'the same again'. But if such a strategy is fundamental to MacNeice's critique of evasion, 'The Slow Starter' (*Solstices*) carries it further. The entire parable is based on what words and phrases keep up their sleeve:

> A watched clock never moves, they said:
> Leave it alone and you'll grow up.
> Nor will the sulking holiday train
> Start sooner if you stamp your feet.
> He left the clock to go its way;
> The whistle blew, the train went gay.

By the end of the poem the comforting proverbial formula has both disproved itself and come to full metaphorical life:

> Oh you have had your chance, It said;
> Left it alone and it was one.
> Who said a watched clock never moves?
> Look at it now. Your chance was I.
> He turned and saw the accusing clock
> Race like a torrent round a rock.

This typically decodes what 'It', some impersonal force, is really saying. Similarly, 'Birthright' (*The Burning Perch*) constructs an emblem from the word 'nightmare', and twists another proverb into sinister omen: 'My gift horse looked me in the mouth'. Since 'cliché' straddles modern slang and ancient lore, *Solstices* renews MacNeice's linguistic communion with 'the popular imagination' in both its contemporary and traditional manifestations. Thus, 'Indoor Sports' makes good the promise of *Modern Poetry* to draw on the jargon of sport or games; while 'The Riddle' finds parabolic resonance in the perennial verbal game of childhood:

> But now the cook is dead and the cooking, no doubt, electric,
> No room for draught or dream, for child or mouse,
> Though we, in another place, still put ourselves the question:
> What *is* it that goes round and round the house?

But MacNeice is also capable of inventing his own riddles (e.g. the gnomic 'Indoor Sports' and 'Sleeping Winds'). He renews the popular imagination itself by confounding its ancient and modern idioms, by making the proverbial riddling and the riddling proverbial: 'If you want to die you will have to pay for it.'

'Idle Talk' takes a more cheerful view of what is latent in language:

> Shop-talk, club-talk, cliché, slang –
> The wind that makes the dead leaf fall
> Can also make the live leaf dance . . .

The last three quatrains of this poem return to the linguistic Garden of Eden evoked by 'When We Were Children', and restore the cliché 'I love you' to its primal freshness. The revitalized cliché, whatever subtext it brings to light, is fundamental to MacNeice's poetic recovery. The mechanically picturesque speech of *Autumn Sequel* had travestied his genuine demotic inspiration. Now he strikes new strata of that inspiration, new tensions between its surfaces and depths. Colour and meaning embark on a second, perhaps maturer, marriage. (The next chapter includes a consideration of how cliché and refrain develop their functions in *The Burning Perch*.) 'Idle Talk', which combines literary theory and practice, marks an aesthetic growth-point. It relishes poetry's seemingly casual sources in 'Anecdote, limerick, tittle-tattle, chestnut'; and, like 'Homage to Clichés', sees in linguistic behaviour a metaphor for human behaviour in general:

> And, come full circle, the chestnut candles
> Abide the spark of tapered wit,
> While the rotten compost of hackneyed phrase
> Reprieves the captive, feeds the future.
>
> For, whether to find oneself or find
> Those other selves through whom one lives,
> The little words that get in the way
> Can also pave the way for a wish.

This reconceived identification between language and life both affirms and proves the possibility of revelation, 'the live leaf', defying the weight of habit or tradition. Further, it celebrates the revitalized cliché, poetry itself, and the revival of MacNeice's creative powers.

VI
'In Need of Myth'

I

Two of the books so far written about MacNeice focus on his attitude to 'belief'. But whereas Terence Brown (in *Sceptical Vision*) concludes that MacNeice's poetry embodies 'a creative scepticism', William T. McKinnon (in *Apollo's Blended Dream*) starts from the premiss that the dominant concepts which condition the poetry are: 'firstly, his deep and abiding awareness of the poet's need for belief, and, secondly, his equally strong and conscious awareness of the need to find the forms . . . appropriate to the creative expression of this belief'. The disagreement need not be paradoxical. Or rather, MacNeice may deal creatively in larger paradoxes than either critical formulation allows. In any case we should be wary, as he was, of putting the philosophical cart before the artistic horse.

Even at Oxford metaphysics for MacNeice 'was not something cold and abstract; it was an account of reality, but an artistic account, not a scientific one' (*SAF*, p. 119). MacNeice's Oxford 'liking for metaphysics', which he acknowledges as a conditioning factor, was never quite as 'dead' as he later maintained (*MP*, p. 89). This made 'blowing the bugles over the metaphysicians' a recurrently necessary self-censorship, part of his quarrel with himself, part of his rhetoric. When metaphysical speculation slips the leash of artistry the result is something like 'The Stygian Banks'. Being a poet interested in 'metaphysical meaning', in our 'whence and whither', is not the same thing as being a metaphysician. MacNeice saw more and more clearly that neither belief, nor the 'world-view' he once hoped metaphysics would bestow, is a straightforward matter for the poet. He accepts that Yeats's 'integrity' survives the possibility that he 'faked his beliefs because he so much *wanted to believe*' (*PWBY*, p. 196). His own poetry's circling around questions of belief seems inseparable from its other antinomies, and also from its belief in itself. Belief is an element in MacNeice's total dialectic or drama; and to this, in *Solstices* and *The Burning Perch*, parable adds new metaphysical dimensions.

MacNeice's concern with belief was in part a product of the 1930s. During that decade writers sought not only political but spiritual validation from authorities outside themselves. In *The Will to Believe*, his study of six thirties novelists, Richard Johnstone draws the following conclusions:

> The thirties are characterized now as an age of belief. It is a sceptic's phrase, applied with hindsight by those who are sadder and wiser. It is a phrase which implies a corollary, a succeeding age of disillusionment, from which we look back at the naivety of earlier days. As such phrases go, it is accurate enough, but it also over-simplifies. People do not as a rule move clearly and sharply from idealism to scepticism, from belief to disillusionment. It might be more accurate to say that the two states exist simultaneously, engaged in a continuing battle for the upper hand. Naive idealism is only one aspect of the thirties . . . A reason why religious belief – Waugh and Greene's Catholicism, Isherwood's Vedanta – survived the thirties while political commitment as a rule did not, is that religious beliefs more easily allowed scepticism and faith to co-exist . . . The novels which now seem truer to the thirties, and to the problems of embarking, not altogether willingly, on the twentieth century, are those which reveal a readiness to confront the sheer difficulty of it all.

MacNeice perhaps deserves all-round credit, since he confronted 'the sheer difficulty of it all' with reference both to politics and to broadly religious issues. Indeed, his discussions of belief interestingly decline to distinguish between cause and creed, while always distinguishing between belief and idolatries. In *Modern Poetry* he applauds belief as he applauds subject matter: 'the fact that beliefs are increasing among poets should conduce to a wider, more fertile, and possibly a major poetry'. However, he goes on to recommend an arm's-length relation to all ideologies: 'But, *for the poet*, any belief, any creed (and beliefs and creeds tend to be *a priori*) should be compromised with his own individual observation' (p. 201). Yeats enlarged his conception of how belief fertilizes art:

> Poets of my generation, who distrust *a priori* methods, tend to found – or think they found – their own beliefs and their own moral principles on evidence. These beliefs and principles are, in their opinion, of the utmost importance to their poetry. So they are, but not necessarily because they are the 'right' beliefs. Poetry gains body from beliefs, and the more suited the belief is to the poet, the healthier his poetry; one poet can thrive on pantheism and another on Christianity; Housman *as a poet* flourished on beliefs the opposite of Browning's. It is not the absolute, or objective, validity of a belief that vindicates the poetry; it is a gross over-simplification to maintain that a right belief makes a poem good and a wrong belief makes a poem bad. First, beliefs are not so easily sorted out into merely right and merely wrong; secondly, by the time a belief is embodied in a poem, it has suffered a biochemical change, has become blended inextricably with mood, picture, and drama.
> (*PWBY*, pp. 196–7)

As we have seen, the war confirmed MacNeice's distrust of the *a priori*, his preference for following 'an ideal that is always developing', while he yet insisted: 'to shun dogma does not mean to renounce belief'. Thus the Note to *Autumn Journal* ('I have certain beliefs . . . which I have refused to abstract from their context') finds a more emphatic echo in the Introductory Note to *The Dark Tower*:

> In an age which precludes the simple and militant faith of a Bunyan, belief (whether consciously formulated or not) still remains a *sine qua non* of the creative writer. I have my beliefs and they permeate *The Dark Tower*. But do not ask me what Ism it illustrates or what Solution it offers. You do not normally ask for such things in the single-plane work; why should they be forced upon something much more complex? 'Why, look you now, how unworthy a thing you make of me!' What is life *useful* for anyway? (p. 22)

Belief for MacNeice became increasingly plural and diffused: Yeatsian 'system against chaos'. In 'What I Believe' (1953) he declared: 'What I do believe is that, as a human being, it is my duty to make patterns and to contribute to order – good patterns and a good order.' If, like Yeats, he partly believed in belief itself, common to all his writings on the subject is a toughly irreducible scorn for utilitarian philosophies: 'What is life *useful* for anyway?' 'Life – let alone art – cannot be assessed purely in terms of utility . . . The faith in the *value* of living is a mystical faith' (*PWBY*, p. 16). Another irreducible credo, one relevant to *The Burning Perch*, is aphoristically stated in *The Strings are False*: 'If Nil is a word it can't be nil' (p. 109).

The word 'duty' reverberates in 'What I Believe', reminding us that MacNeice was not only a child of his age but a child of the rectory. Richard Johnstone notes that 'Communism and Catholicism were increasingly singled out . . . as the alternative cures for the sickness of a generation'. (Hence the joke about writers choosing between the Communist Church and the Catholic Party.) However, in the case of religion as of politics Ireland placed MacNeice at a special angle to collective trends. If 'the intransigence of my own / Countrymen' made absolute political commitment unattractive, exposure to religious Ireland ruled out the conversions of a Waugh, Greene or Auden. On the one hand, Catholicism (or Anglo-Catholicism) could never have the exotic, élitist appeal it held for his English literary contemporaries; on the other, MacNeice had a more powerful brand of Protestantism breathing down his neck. Even today few writers from Ireland inhabit the kind of post-religious climate that makes orthodox religion an inspiring mythic option. But by the same token it was possible for MacNeice to feel the death of God as acutely as Thomas Hardy had felt it. He says in 'When I Was Twenty-One': 'Having been brought up in a traditionally religious family and having, true to my period, reacted violently against the Christian dogma and, to some extent too, against the Christian ethic, I felt morally naked and spiritually hungry.' Chapter I indicated how some 'petrifying' aspects of Ulster Protestantism contributed to MacNeice's fear of the dark. Nevertheless his relation to his religious background was by no means wholly negative. E. R.

Dodds observes: 'He never to my knowledge claimed to be a Christian, though he made free use of Christian imagery, but the questions that troubled him all his life were at bottom religious questions.' In *Modern Poetry* MacNeice himself testifies that 'from a very early age I was fascinated by the cadences and imagery of the Bible' (p. 35). This aesthetic influence is itself significant (and partly interprets MacNeice's sense of affinity with George Herbert), but Bible, Prayer Book and Hymn Book also permeate the deepest strata of his poetry. Thus MacNeice's dialectic about belief can be read as a dialogue with his father. 'The Truisms' in *Solstices* begins by establishing the grounds for a life-long argument:

> His father gave him a box of truisms
> Shaped like a coffin, then his father died;
> The truisms remained on the mantelpiece
> As wooden as the playbox they had been packed in
> Or that other his father skulked inside.

Bishop MacNeice's death in 1942 had brought the dialogue closer to the surface. 'The Kingdom' celebrates him as 'One who believed and practised and whose life / Presumed the Resurrection'. The poem continues, faint but pursuing: 'What that means / He may have felt he knew.' (MacNeice never forgot his father's happiness on Easter Sunday.) 'The Strand' more explicitly suggests the son following, at a metaphorical distance, in the footsteps of the father who represents greater solidity in the context of faith as well as of Ireland: 'A square black figure whom the horizon understood'.

Besides never flirting with Catholicism, MacNeice deprecated the resort to Eastern mysticism by writers such as Isherwood and Huxley. If 'going muzzily religious' ('Broken Windows') was out, it was also emphatically 'no go the Yogi-Man'. His objections were not merely rationalist. (MacNeice always discriminates very finely between what should be rendered unto reason and what should not.) His consciousness of a rigorous Christianity, including the Bishop's courageous stance in sectarian Belfast, seems to have stiffened him against all kinds of muzziness, even if it did not tempt him to conform. Hence the fact that 'duty', 'conscience' and other terms which belong to 'the Christian ethic' remain alive in his poetry and prose. Indeed 'The Creditor', the very first poem in the *Collected Poems*, consists of a dialectic between 'debts to God' and 'lulling' reverie. This contest between religion and art antedates the thirties conflict between commitment and aestheticism. Some of MacNeice's central imaginative preoccupations, his interest in mortality (akin to Hardy's) as well as in ethics, devolve from a Christian framework whose theology and terminology he continually revises: 'Through a glass greenly'; 'this morn / They say, interpret it your own way, Christ is born'; 'hark the herald angels / Beg for copper coins'. MacNeice's pervasive quotation from religious sources does not stop at idioms, cadences and imagery, but affects structure: his adaptations of liturgy (several 'Prayers', 'Bar-room Matins'), his sermonizing touches. Nor was it only the secular variety of parable that appealed to him. The impact of the doctrinal type can be felt in a poem like 'The Slow Starter' as well as in 'Jehu' or 'The Tree of Guilt'. And his admiration for *Pilgrim's Progress*, elaborated in *Varieties of Parable*, influenced MacNeice's parabolic use of the journey and of 'abstractions' made 'concrete' (*VP*, p. 45).

In proportion to the rise of parable, religiously inscribed poems multiply in *Solstices*. 'Sunday in the Park' is an example of how MacNeice's late satire exploits Christian ideas and symbols. Some of the chilling stasis in the poem seems to derive from moral paralysis, from the absence of a cohering vision, from 'loss' of the knowledge of good and evil:

> Here is Sunday:
> And on the seventh day He rested. The Tree
> Forgets both good and evil in irony.

Here MacNeice's 'irony' runs less against the grain of Christianity than it does in 'Sunday Morning'. The heavier irony of 'Jericho' takes an Old Testament text as a stick to beat modern sins which cry out for divine punishment:

> And the sun stood still above the Ministry of Defence
> And Joshua remembered Moses.
> Neither sense nor conscience stirred,

Having been ultimately deterred,
And the Tables of the Law were broken again.

However, the irony in both cases may cover the Almighty's inertia too. The Bible also plays a more positive role in *Solstices*. What MacNeice terms the 'poems of acceptance (even of joy)' sometimes fuse the myth of Eden with his personal mythology. 'Good Dream', punctuated by the book of Genesis, ends:

'And God
Said Let there be light'.
His usual room
Has lost its usual walls and found
Four walls of sky, incredible blue
Enclosing incredible green enclosing
Her, none other.
Completely awake.

'Idle Talk' and 'The Wall' also end in Edenic circumstances, with a similar sense of barriers – between people, between here and the beyond – dissolving in a garden. A window opening, a wall vanishing, a house invaded by its garden (all of which go back concretely as well as theologically to Carrickfergus rectory) recur in the visionary moments of MacNeice's poetry. In these the religious reinforces the secular rather than vice versa. 'Good Dream' is an allegory of love, drawing on physical as well as cosmic birth. Similarly, the last line of 'The Wall', 'The first garden. The last', is ambiguous. The title of 'Apple Blossom' heretically implies that eating the apple was not a Fall but a flowering. MacNeice makes biblical (and Miltonic) concepts serve earthly revelation, the revelation of earth:

For the next ocean is the first ocean
And the last ocean is the first ocean
And, however often the sun may rise,
A new thing dawns upon our eyes.

For the last blossom is the first blossom
And the first blossom is the best blossom
And when from Eden we take our way
The morning after is the first day.

The protagonist of 'The Truisms' also comes round not quite full circle. This is not a poem of conversion, but a poem that recognizes the transmutations of spiritual inheritance:

> Then he left home, left the truisms behind him
> Still on the mantelpiece, met love, met war,
> Sordor, disappointment, defeat, betrayal,
> Till through disbeliefs he arrived at a house
> He could not remember seeing before,
>
> And he walked straight in; it was where he had come from
> And something told him the way to behave.
> He raised his hand and blessed his home;
> The truisms flew and perched on his shoulders
> And a tall tree sprouted from his father's grave.

Some of MacNeice's poetry, certainly his imaginative tension between 'truisms' and 'disbeliefs', sprouted from his father's grave. Their dialogue hovers over the Tree and the Word. However, the knowledge enshrined in the poetic epiphanies is not essentially Christian, just as the Word ultimately resides in words. Although MacNeice possessed a 'mystical faith' in the value of living, and allowed himself still more mystical licence with respect to the West of Ireland, he never took any final religious vows that would close down his artistic options. His important distinction between the poet and 'the mystic proper', also perhaps between himself and his father, holds good:

> [Yeats] was like Lancelot who nearly saw the Grael. He believed in the Grael, *divining* its presence (to use Plato's metaphor), he made great efforts to achieve direct vision. But it was perhaps just because he lacked this direct vision that he was able to write poetry. Would not Lancelot have been able to give a better account of the Quest than Galahad? Galahad, I feel, would have forgotten the road in the goal achieved and have lost his human feelings in that superhuman experience. (*PWBY*, p. 25)

'The Blasphemies', a version of MacNeice's career to date, is central to *Solstices*. It interprets the book's religious background and metaphysical foreground. Like 'The Truisms', 'The

Blasphemies' narrates a history of negotiations with belief, negotiations at once personal and artistic. Despite the poem's autobiographical basis, it dramatizes a representative dilemma of the twentieth-century writer, twentieth-century man – and perhaps MacNeice also still speaks for his dispersed generation. These shadows from his Ulster childhood haunt others too:

> The sin against the Holy . . . though what
> He wondered was it? Cold in his bed
> He thought: If I think those words I know
> Yet must not be thinking – Come to the hurdle
> And I shall be damned through thinking Damn –
> But Whom? But no! Those words are unthinkable;
> Damn anyone else, but once I – No,
> Here lies the unforgivable blasphemy.
> So pulling the cold sheets over his head
> He swore to himself he had not thought
> Those words he knew but never admitted.
> To be damned at seven years old was early.

In the second stanza the protagonist, 'his Who's Who / No longer cosmic', has become 'a gay blasphemer'. The punning inversion of hell-haunted child denotes 'violent' reaction aganst petrifaction. However, by the end of the stanza this is firmly placed as over-reaction. Ironically something has been lost along with that early intensity and its cosmology:

> And what is a joke about God if you do not
> Accept His existence? Where is the blasphemy?
> No Hell at seventeen feels empty.

'Rising thirty' the protagonist graduates from iconoclasm to a substitute for religion, equivalent to MacNeice's humanism of the late 1930s, which yet leaves certain hungers unsatisfied:

> So humanism was all and the only
> Sin was the sin against the Human –
> But you could not call it Ghost for that
> Was merely emotive; the only – you could not

Call it sin for that was emotive –
The only failure was not to face
The facts. But at thirty what are the facts?

The fourth stanza begins 'Ten years later, in need of myth . . .' and takes autobiography up to 1947, *The Dark Tower*, and the creative problems of that period. Section 2 of this chapter will consider how parable satisfies the mythic needs of MacNeice's poetry. But the perspective from which 'The Blasphemies' reviews the past (though itself of course not a final judgement but part of an evolving dialectic) should be complemented by poems from the decades in question, which explicitly address the issue of pattern in the universe. Such poems as 'Train to Dublin', 'Wolves', 'Entirely', 'Plant and Phantom', 'London Rain', 'The Dowser', 'Precursors', 'Mutations', 'The Cromlech' and 'Plurality' spotlight the metaphysics – and anti-metaphysics – at work elsewhere.

Previous chapters have discussed various positive patterns at which MacNeice's poetry arrives: variousness itself, the seizing of flux, timeless love, 'Hatred of hatred, assertion of human values', Utopias, wartime empiricism, western visions. Indeed, this list suggests a correlation between following a developing ideal and artistic range. In *Poems* (1935) 'Train to Dublin' and 'Wolves' fend off the hazards of dogma on a wider front than 'To a Communist' and 'The Individualist Speaks'. As already noted (see page 14) 'Train to Dublin' explores perhaps the fundamental metaphysical paradox that troubles the conscience of MacNeice's poetry: how can pattern be achieved without stasis, without falsely systematizing, without doing violence to what a letter of 1930 calls 'Lots of lovely particulars'? The poem contrasts 'gathering my mind up in my fist' with life's own fluid 'repatterning'. This approximates to MacNeice's account of being drawn 'two ways' in philosophy: 'I wanted the world to be One, to be permanent, the incarnation of an absolute Idea . . . At the same time any typical monistic system [i.e. based on Oneness] appeared hopelessly static, discounting Becoming as mere illusion and hamstringing human action' (*SAF*, pp. 124–5). 'Wolves' even disowns the categories of flux and permanence:

The tide comes in and goes out again, I do not want
To be always stressing either its flux or its permanence,
I do not want to be a tragic or philosophic chorus
But to keep my eye only on the nearer future
And after that let the sea flow over us.

On the other hand, 'Wolves' is partly an attack on the thirties illusion that any conceptualization or shared ideology can avert 'the wolves of water / Who howl along our coast'. And 'Train to Dublin' incorporates into its own synthesis the prospect of others:

I would like to give you more but I cannot hold
This stuff within my hands and the train goes on;
I know that there are further syntheses to which,
As you have perhaps, people at last attain
And find that they are rich and breathing gold.

However, the 'further syntheses' seem modelled on an interpenetration of life and art ('breathing gold') rather than on philosophical solutions. William T. McKinnon notices 'MacNeice's hostility towards any metaphysical system that postulated or implied a division between the actual world of phenomenal time, space, and experience, and any transcendental principle, where the former was regarded as a mere reflection of the latter, or as a phenomenal creation apart from its creator or prime mover'. But in a sense poetry was itself the answer to the problem of monism versus pluralism or of the ideal versus the real. He wrote in 1935: 'We [poets] want just enough a priori to make us ruthless so that when we meet the inrush of a posteriori (commonly called "life") we can sweep away the vastly greater part of it and let the rest body out our potential pattern; by the time this is done, it will be not only a new but the first pattern of its kind and not particularly ours' (*SCLM*, p. 43). The marriage of form and matter joins what philosophy sunders. At one pole MacNeice's poetry dissolves metaphysical pattern into its larger unity, as at another it dissolves social pattern. All this is true of *Autumn Journal*'s rich syntheses, which reconcile core and circumference, and gather up the mind while going with the flow.

The 'empiricism' that 'Broken Windows' expounds developed from the balances struck in *Autumn Journal*. 'London Rain', written on the brink of war, fantastically schematizes the European conflict into one between God and No-God:

> Under God we can reckon
> On pardon when we fall
> But if we are under No-God
> Nothing will matter at all,
> Arson and rape and murder
> Must count for nothing at all.

But this 'metaphysics' betrays its own casuistry and evasion (compare section XIII of *Autumn Journal*):

> The argument was wilful,
> The alternatives untrue,
> We need no metaphysics
> To sanction what we do
> Or to muffle us in comfort
> From what we did not do.

The poem goes on to define more satisfactory – and empirical – consciousness in terms which unite flux with human action (as does *Autumn Journal*), and which ultimately belong to poetry. In this climactic stanza, refrain, rhythm and rhyme reproduce the energy of the 'maker' working on the 'given':

> Whether the living river
> Began in bog or lake,
> The world is what was given,
> The world is what we make
> And we only can discover
> Life in the life we make.

'Entirely' denies that a single key to the universe exists, and again defines the available insights in terms appropriate to its own cadence: 'All we know is the splash of words in passing / And falling twigs of song.' Written at the end of the war, 'The Cromlech' further endorses the 'given' by adding 'glory', by attacking 'Extracters and abstracters', and by preaching on the text of 'Snow'. MacNeice juxtaposes, and refuses to do more than juxtapose, young lovers and a prehistoric stone structure, thus insisting on distinct identity in time as well as in space:

Tom is here, Tessy is here
At this point in a given year
With all this hour's accessories,
A given glory – and to look
That gift-horse in the mouth will prove
Or disprove nothing of their love
Which is as sure intact a fact,
Though young and supple, as what stands
Obtuse and old, in time congealed,
Behind them as they mingle hands –
Self-contained, unexplained,
The cromlech in the clover field.

'Plurality' (1940), which assembles a number of these ideas, is itself only partially saved from 'abstraction' by the swing of its hexameter couplets. The following repudiation of monism uses the image of snow in the same critical manner as 'To a Communist':

The modern monist too castrates, negates our lives
And nothing that we do, make or become survives,
His terror of confusion freezes the flowing stream
Into mere illusion, his craving for supreme
Completeness means he chokes each orifice with tight
Plaster as he evokes a dead ideal of white
All-white Universal, refusing to allow
Division or dispersal – Eternity is now
And Now is therefore numb, a fact he does not see . . .

'Plant and Phantom' emphasizes the impossibility of getting the hang of it entirely by posing the riddle of man in cryptic syntax which anticipates the later poetry: 'Man: a flutter of pages, / Leaves in the Sybil's cave . . .' However, just as 'Plurality' commends the human effort, though always incomplete, to be 'conscious', so 'Plant and Phantom' approves man's neo-religious compulsion to solve his own riddle:

Who felt with his hands in empty
Air for the Word and did not

> Find it but felt the aura,
> Dew on the skin, could not forget it.

In all these poems MacNeice's perspectives on 'pattern' approach Yeats's conclusion: 'Man can embody truth but he cannot know it.' There may be tacit identification in this summing up of Yeats: 'Although from one angle a romantic individualist, even an anarchist, he had always had a desire to docket the universe' (*PWBY*, p. 112); and also in this account of how Yeats's poetry outsmarts his philosophy: 'that he knew how any . . . diagram must be unjust to its concrete subject is proved by those poems which are professedly on the same theme; here what was static becomes dynamic, what was abstract concrete' (p. 117).

One belief of MacNeice's which led him to distrust the *a priori* and the 'dead ideal' is his belief in finding life through 'surrender', as 'The Sea' puts it, and through 'surprise':

> Surprises keep us living: as when the first light
> Surprised our infant eyes or as when, very small,
> Clutching our parents' hands we toddled down a road
> Where all was blank and windless both to touch and sight
> Had we not suddenly raised our eyes which showed
> The long grass blowing wild on top of the high wall.
> ('Mutations')

In *The Strings are False* (the Appendix written later) MacNeice cites this and other childhood revelations, such as the genesis of 'Round the Corner', as having given him 'a sense of eternity'. He continues:

> This explains perhaps why I have never steered myself much. An American friend once said to me rebukingly: 'You never seem to make any positive choice; you just let things happen to you.' But the things that happen to one often seem better than the things one chooses. Even in writing poetry, which is something I did early choose to do, the few poems or passages which I find wear well have something of accident about them (the poems I did not intend to write) or, to put it more pretentiously, seem 'given'. So Magilligan Strand was like falling in love. For such occasions the word 'falling' is right;

> one does not step into love any more than one steps asleep – or awake. For awake, like asleep, is what one falls, and to keep falling awake seems to me the salt of life much more than existentialist defiance. We cannot of course live by Keats's Negative Sensibility alone, we must all, in E. M. Forster's phrase, use 'telegrams and anger'; all the same what I feel makes life worth living is not the clever scores but the surrenders – it may be to the life-quickening urge of an air-raid, to nonsense talked by one's friends, to a girl on top of the Empire State building, to the silence of a ruined Byzantine church, to woods, or weirs, or to heat dancing on a gravelled path, to music, drink or the smell of turf smoke, to the first view of the Atlantic or to the curve of a strand which seems to stretch to nowhere or everywhere and to ages before and after the combustion engine which defiled it. (p. 220)

That marvellous passage ties in the visionary moments of MacNeice's poetry with its origins and methods. His moments of vision are not of course unique in their religious valuation of certain earthly phenomena. However, their intensity has points of contact with 'presuming the Resurrection'. 'The Return' uses 'Bethlehem is desolate' as a symbol of war, then answers desolation with a mixture of pagan and Christian resurrectionism:

> The acclamation of earth's returning daughter,
> Jonquils out of hell, and after
> Hell the imperative of joy, the dancing
> Fusillade of sunlight on the water.

As 'Easter Returns' in *Visitations* says, 'the myth returns, the stone / Is rolled away once more'. The apostolic 'Precursors' 'carry an emerald lamp behind their faces', and the poem shares with 'The Dowser' (water-diviner) a baptismal image of powerfully regenerative water. 'The Dowser', like 'The Return' a wartime parable, also blends sacred and profane ingredients to convey the 'inkling' of revelation, of some Messianic advent or resurrection. The surprise at (and of) the poem's conclusion again symbolizes the redemptive principle as a burst of water, light and flowers (compare 'Mayfly'):

A well? A mistake somewhere . . .
More of a tomb . . . Anyhow we backed away
From the geyser suddenly of light that erupted, sprayed
Rocketing over the sky azaleas and gladioli.

MacNeice's poetry believes in divination if not in the divine.

2

On one level the fourth stanza of 'The Blasphemies' might seem to query the approach of a poem like 'The Dowser'. It asks whether 'symbols' lose their force if not sustained by 'faith':

Ten years later, in need of myth,
He thought: I can use my childhood symbols
Divorced from their context, Manger and Cross
Could do very well for Tom Dick and Harry –
Have we not all of us been in a war
So have we not carried call it a cross
Which was never our fault? Yet how can a cross
Be never your fault? The words of the myth,
Now merely that and no longer faith,
Melt in his hands . . .

However, by the last stanza ('Forty to fifty') the issues have become still more complex. On the one hand, the protagonist's phase of reaction to and against religion has run its course. On the other, his original question still hangs mysteriously in the air:

For himself
He was not Tom or Dick or Harry,
Let alone God, he was merely fifty,
No one and nowhere else, a walking
Question but no more cheap than any
Question or quest is cheap. The sin
Against the Holy Ghost – What is it?

Like 'The Truisms', 'The Blasphemies' revisits and revises its starting-point, but it ends with a question mark rather than an epiphany. These complementary poems stake out the dialectic of

Solstices and *The Burning Perch*, a dialectic which renews old obsessions by casting them into parabolic forms.

MacNeice's continuing 'need of myth' in the 1950s was again a double-pronged affair of aesthetic needs and faith. An expansion of his mythological horizons helped him to reconcile the two, to avoid the fork that impales the blasphemer in stanza four. His later parables have digested his radio work on legendary and folk materials from Nordic, English and Irish sources. Nor should his classical hinterland be forgotten. However, after 'Dark Age Glosses' such influences are more structurally than literally present. 'Charon' does not so much prove the rule by exception as prove how naturally myth lends itself to MacNeice's vision. He says of *Solstices*: 'when my central image is a windscreen wiper, I feel myself just as mythopoeic as if I were writing about the Grael' (*SCLM*, p. 224). Perhaps his increased mythopoeia confirms an Irish literary leaning formerly constrained by keeping off the Yeatsian grass. His friendship with the mythopoeic Dylan Thomas may also be relevant. MacNeice found Thomas, whom he exempted from his strictures on the so-called 'Neo-Romantics' of the 1940s, a stimulating rather than irritating anti-type of 'the thirties poet'. In *Autumn Sequel* Thomas figures as a kind of Muse, and MacNeice's prose tributes relish him for being 'nearer to the folk world than to the bookish world', and for possessing a rare 'sense of value, a faith in something that is simultaneously physical and spiritual' (*SCLM*, pp. 183–8). By strengthening his mythic access to the archetypal MacNeice in a sense resumed the agenda of 'Eclogue by a Five-barred Gate'. His last radio play *Persons from Porlock*, which ends with a meeting between its painter-hero and death, uses underground cave systems as a metaphor for regions the artist must explore.

How far MacNeice had reversed some axioms of the 1930s can be gauged from his admission in *Varieties of Parable*: 'In the 1930s we used to say that the poet should contain the journalist; now I would tend more often to use "contain" in the sense of control or limit' (p. 8). Containing journalism meant limiting discursiveness as well as realism, 'statement' as well as 'information'. But MacNeice's later poetry owes its greater economy not only to cuts in volubility but to positive formal strategies.

Narrative, symbol, syntax and idiom now do most of the talking. He describes the short poems in *Visitations* as 'relying more on syntax and bony feature than on bloom or frill or the floating image' (*SCLM*, p. 211). His didactic and philosophical impulses follow discursiveness underground. Whereas in *The Poetry of W. B. Yeats* MacNeice sees the artist as 'simultaneously putting his own question and making his own answer to it' (p. 26), in *Varieties of Parable* the emphasis alters: 'the nearest one gets to an answer is in the sheer phrasing of the question' (p. 124). Dwelling on the question may take you further than rushing towards an answer (as some thirties writers did): 'What *is* it that goes round and round the house?' 'The sin / Against the Holy Ghost – What is it?' It was Beckett who prompted MacNeice's remark about 'the sheer phrasing of the question'. His responsiveness to the cast of Beckett's imagination has something to do with the Irish Protestant background they share (MacNeice always stresses Beckett's Irishness). In a *New Statesman* article of 1961 he wrote of *Waiting for Godot* as 'a poetic play', one issuing from the concerns of a lyric poet, in terms that fit *The Burning Perch*: 'articulating (which is not quite the word) questions that have no answer – but merely to put these questions is a worthwhile gesture'. There is also clear identification in his insistence that Beckett is essentially not an Absurdist, but on the side of system against chaos, 'a religious writer':

> Just as the absence of God implies the need of God and therefore the presence of at least something spiritual in man, so to have failed in living implies certain values in living, however much Beckett's characters may curse and blaspheme against it and behave like clowns in a clownish universe. As with any other blasphemy, the other side of the coin is an act of homage. (*VP*, p. 142)

So a series of blasphemies can be a kind of progress. 'The Blasphemies' makes explicit the structures of question and quest behind many other poems.

For MacNeice parable is an elastic mode, although not infinitely so. It involves, among other things: 'the creation of a special world', 'a strong spiritual, or indeed a mystical element', preoccupation with 'the problem of identity', an Everyman protagonist, belief or a world view, a quality akin to dreams and therefore to unconscious experience (*VP*, pp. 76–9). Psychologically, parable deals with 'the inner life of man'; sociologically, it is 'imbued with the true inner feel of its period'. All of the above applies, for instance, to *The Faerie Queene*. Perhaps MacNeice's most fundamental point about parable's formal organization is that 'all allegory involves symbolism, and in proportion as symbolism becomes developed and coherent it tends towards allegory' (p. 67). This might be said of 'Nature Notes' or 'Sleeping Winds'. MacNeice objected to the purism about symbolism left over from early Modernist theory. He approved Rosemond Tuve's observation in *A Reading of George Herbert* that 'metaphysical wit and concord of unlikes in an image is precisely the operation, much condensed, of the old (and maligned) allegorical mode of writing'. Always critical of Modernist concentration on Donne, in *Varieties of Parable* (which he thought of calling *From Spenser to Beckett*) he is anxious to show that Spenser and Herbert have something to teach contemporary poets.

A significant feature of *The Burning Perch* as compared with *Solstices* is a rise in the ratio of 'dream logic'. Dreams had been waiting a long time to play as shaping a role in MacNeice's aesthetic as they did in his life. Even in *Solstices* 'Bad Dream' seems over-explicitly titled and executed. Of course nightmare sensations and images pervade his earlier poetry, and the 'Hangman's Gate' sequence in section XV of *Autumn Journal* highlights the fact that they also perform structural functions, especially when phantasmagoria is called for. However, MacNeice's critical ideas about dreams ran ahead of his practice. Thus an essay on Malory (1936) begins by likening the effect of *Morte d'Arthur* to a 'dream becoming palpably more substantial', making its 'dialectic . . . concrete' (*SCLM*, pp. 45–6). In *Modern Poetry*, discussing Auden's use of 'dream technique', he says: 'In dreams the hierarchies of life break down' (p. 106). This describes what happens in 'Variation on Heraclitus' or 'Reflections'. As with Alice's experiences, the norms of perception and perspective radically change. In 'Hold-up', another poem of stasis and asyndeton, the everyday world has become more thoroughly paranormal than in 'Sunday in the Park'. This nightmare traffic-jam brings to a dream-logical conclusion images in 'Morning Sun' and 'The Glacier':

> The bubbles in the football pools
> Went flat, the hot news froze, the dates
> They could not keep were dropped like charred
> Matches, the girls no longer flagged
> Their sex, besides the code was lost,
> The engine stalled, a tall glass box
> On the pavement held a corpse in pickle
> His ear still cocked, and no one spoke . . .

Three poems in *The Burning Perch* which contrast in their use of dream logic are 'Flower Show', 'The Introduction' and 'Soap Suds'. 'Flower Show', instead of piling on macabre details as 'Bad Dream' does, turns a single nightmare image into a strong symbol whose grotesqueness is emblematic of a denatured, dehumanized environment:

> Squidlike, phallic or vulvar, hypnotic, idiotic, oleaginous,
> Fanged or whaleboned, wattled or balding, brimstone or cold
> As trout or seaweed, these blooms, ogling or baneful, all
> Keep him in their blind sights; he tries to stare them down
> But they are too many, too unreal, their aims are one, the controlled
> Aim of a firing party.

'The Introduction' presents the story of older-man-meets-younger-girl as an encounter in 'a green grave', mocked by a chorus of sinister dream presences: 'Crawly crawly / Went the twigs above their heads and beneath / The grass beneath their feet the larvae / Split themselves laughing'. 'Soap Suds' moves between ordinary consciousness and a nightmare croquet game (shades of *Alice* again): 'And the grass has grown head-high and an angry voice cries Play!' The people in all these poems find themselves at the mercy of apparitions, voices, metamorphoses, and sudden transitions, which raise questions about the world they inhabit. 'Charon', 'The Taxis' and 'After the Crash' are more completely constructed by dream logic. Their protagonists suffer more extremely the dream experience of being neither in touch nor in control: 'We moved through London, / We could see the pigeons through the glass but failed / To hear their rumours of wars' ('Charon'). The figure in 'The Taxis' has no control over his identity, his self-definition, in the same way as Alice has difficulties about getting her existence verified in *Through the Looking-Glass*:

> As for the fourth taxi, he was alone
> Tra-la when he hailed it but the cabby looked
> Through him and said: 'I can't tra-la well take
> So many people, not to speak of the dog.'

'After the Crash' depicts a post-holocaust landscape in which the hierarchies of life have comprehensively broken down:

> When he came to he knew
> Time must have passed because
> The asphalt was high with hemlock
> Through which he crawled to his crash
> Helmet and found it no more
> Than his wrinkled hand what it was.

Terence Brown comments: 'The "because" here is quite illogical. The asphalt high with hemlock does not necessarily mean time has passed' (*Sceptical Vision*). Of course Time may have passed in a more absolute sense. What this protagonist sees and 'hears' (including impossibly 'the silence of small blind cats / Debating whether to pounce') suggests terminal throes. The final surreal apparition may imply that no hierarchy exists even to impose a day of judgement or meaningful pattern:

> Then he looked up and marked
> The gigantic scales in the sky,
> The pan on the left dead empty
> And the pan on the right dead empty,
> And knew in the dead, dead calm
> It was too late to die.

If we read these and other poems as a sequence we can perceive the mid-twentieth-century mutation of Spenserian adventures, the mythic shape of the Quest: 'The great majority of folk tales include journeys, sometimes on sea, more often on land, and the quest which in such stories is usually aimed at finding a fortune or a bride can become in other hands the Quest of the Grail or of the City of Zion' (*VP*, p. 12). In the Quest, 'empiricism' finds its natural mythic body. MacNeice of course identified the poet with Lancelot, able to give an 'account of the Quest'. And he said of poetry: 'A poem may be a bridge to the unknown but it is a bridge essentially constructed in terms of the known' (*PWBY*, p. 25). He was not the only poet of his generation to be interested in the Quest or indeed in parabolic methods. Auden's sonnet sequence 'The Quest' (1941) draws on folk motifs:

> He parried every question that they hurled:
> 'What did the Emperor tell you?' 'Not to push?'
> 'What is the greatest wonder of the world?
> 'The bare man Nothing in the Beggar's Bush.'
>
> ('The Hero')

However, as MacNeice says, 'If at times [Auden] is a parabolist, he is not a consistent or sustained one', and in *The Age of Anxiety* he 'gets his effects by enumeration rather than by fusion' (*VP*, pp. 106–7). The same could be said of cantos XIV–XVI of *Autumn Sequel*: an explicit, discursive attempt at the Quest. MacNeice's true parabolic 'fusion' required a deeper absorption of Quest-structure. To this structure the sea quest, especially the *immram* or Irish voyage tale (see page 30) on which he modelled his radio play *The Mad Islands* (1962), also made a contribution. The characteristic feature of such a voyage is that it penetrates the beyond, visiting 'otherworld' islands which might be dream islands, or as MacNeice notes 'parable islands'. A third ingredient in his mythic mix is the Christian-Morality tradition of Everyman.

The plays that MacNeice modelled on Knightly Quest, the *immram* and *Everyman* can help us to interpret the procedures of the later poetry. *The Dark Tower* is of course a crucial prototype. Its opening Announcement states:

> The theme is the ancient but ever-green theme of the Quest – the dedicated adventure; the manner of presentation is that of a

dream – but a dream that is full of meaning. Browning's poem ends with a challenge blown on a trumpet:

> 'And yet
> Dauntless the slughorn to my lips I set
> And blew. "Childe Roland to the Dark Tower came".'

Note well the words 'And yet'. Roland did not have to – he did not wish to – and yet in the end he came to: The Dark Tower. (p. 23)

The play's concept of 'the dedicated adventure' blends the Grail story with MacNeice's belief since the later 1930s that the human spirit must engage with its (mostly self-born) adversaries: 'Minute your gesture but it must be made.' In some ways *The Dark Tower* is a dynamic version of 'Prayer before Birth'. Like all his brothers before him, Roland is groomed to seek and fight the Dragon of the Dark Tower:

> All that we know is there is something there
> Which makes the Dark Tower dark and is the source
> Of evil through the world. It is immortal
> But men must try to kill it – and keep on trying
> So long as we would be human.

He overcomes the temptations of love and a quiet life, lack of faith, doubts as to whether he truly has free will:

> I Roland, the black sheep, the unbeliever –
> Who never did anything of his own free will –
> Will do this now to bequeath free will to others.

The hero of *The Mad Islands* discovers that his avenging Quest has been dedicated to a mistaken goal. But that discovery may itself be an advance and he just manages to continue the voyage (compare the end of 'The Wiper': 'And yet we hold the road'). However, the decline in humanistic faith since *The Dark Tower* seems significant. A feature of the play is the moral lessons to be learned from its parable islands, such as the Island of Progress which eventually explodes. It is not too far-fetched to see the composite Quester of MacNeice's poetry as landing at freakish parable islands – 'Flower Show' is only one island of progress – or coming up against hazards as Roland does. The terrain of 'After the Crash' recalls Roland's last ordeal in the desert. In both plays the hero inhabits a context of voices (internal or external?) advising, criticizing or 'conducting' like those in the poems. This is also the case with MacNeice's modern Everyman in his stage play *One for the Grave* (written in 1958–9). Everyman, his cosmos a TV studio, is interrogated and found wanting by personifications like Free Will, Patria, Conscience and Lucre, by special investigators like the Marxist and the Analyst, and by members of the human family. The manipulative Floor Manager sums up his condition as 'E for earth, V for virus, E for evil, R for ruin, Y for yellow, M for misfit, A for anguish, N for nobody'. However, Free Will and Conscience accompany Everyman to the grave, and the Gravedigger salutes him 'in the name of Life'.

MacNeice was sceptical about Eliot's claim to poetic 'impersonality', arguing that he merely avoided saying 'I'. However, the 'he' of his own later poetry, if an extension of self-dramatization, makes a convincing representative of the human race. Compared with the persona of *Autumn Journal*, the social and metaphysical levels of Everyman's existence are now more finely fused. 'Flower Show' might be society or more universal horrors; the London of 'Charon' includes the London of *Autumn Journal* and of the wartime poems. 'As in Their Time', twelve miniature case studies of the modern Everyman, moves easily from specific social satire to metaphysical imponderables, from the moral to the mythic. *The Burning Perch* develops the tendency in *Visitations* and *Solstices* for poems to imitate the *Everyman* pattern of encapsulating the entire course of human life (e.g. 'The Tree of Guilt', 'Figure of Eight', 'The Slow Starter', 'The Truisms'). 'As in Their Time' cuts it down to *King Lear* in five lines:

> He had clowned it through. Being born
> For either the heights or the depths
> He had bowled his hoop on the level
> Arena: the hoop was a wheel
> Of fire but he clowned it through.

'The Habits', like 'The Slow Starter', updates the Morality tradition, but injects a higher dose of dream panic: 'When they put him in rompers the habits / Fanned out to close in . . .' Everyman's personified habits not only represent life as predetermined, but criticize the conformity and evasion which keep it that way, which rule out the dedicated adventure. The self-criticism of *Autumn Journal* takes on a new form:

> Age became middle: the habits
> Made themselves at home, they were dressed
> In quilted dressing-gowns and carried
> A decanter, a siphon, and a tranquillizer;
> The computer said it was all for the best.

'Soap Suds' shows free will as losing out to habit and time rather than abdicating from the start. The remembered house of childhood is at once vividly concrete and a powerful symbolic microcosm of the world into which we are born:

> This brand of soap has the same smell as once in the big
> House he visited when he was eight: the walls of the bathroom
> open
> To reveal a lawn where a great yellow ball rolls back through a
> hoop
> To rest at the head of a mallet held in the hands of a child.
>
> And these were the joys of that house: a tower with a telescope;
> Two great faded globes, one of the earth, one of the stars;
> A stuffed black dog in the hall; a walled garden with bees;
> A rabbit warren; a rockery; a vine under glass; the sea.

This marvellous double-level writing balances the 'stuffed black dog' against the live rabbits and bees, the enclosed garden and vine against the 'open' sea. Then the balance tilts. The sense of the world, the sunlike ball, at the child's feet, ready to be explored, gives way to the adult's nightmare recognition that the world has controlled him:

> And the grass has grown head-high and an angry voice cries
> Play!

But the ball is lost and the mallet slipped long since from the
hands
Under the running tap that are not the hands of a child.

Praising 'Soap Suds', the poet Hugo Williams has said: 'How did he know it was a *yellow* ball though? No other colour would have done. Only sixteen lines and yet it rolls such a lifetime' (*Poetry Review* vol. 75, no. 3).

But most of the poems which roll Everyman's lifetime, and weigh the balance of free will and fate, are journey poems. 'The Burnt Bridge' (a 'bridge to the Unknown') in *Visitations* is a prototype, close to Malory and *The Dark Tower*, reaching very obviously for the folk tradition just as 'The Tree of Guilt' overtly amalgamates the Morality, folk elements, and romance. MacNeice half-parodies motifs like 'the haunted coombe' and 'birds a-croak', and uses a ballad quatrain. Its more open rhyme-scheme (ABAC) as compared with the quatrain of 'The Tree of Guilt' (AABB) helps to establish a rhythm of Quest which differs from the heavily accentuated rhythm of emblem (both have their subtler successors):

For his long-lost dragon lurked ahead,
Not to be dodged and never napping,
And he knew in his bones he was all but dead,
Yet that death was half the story.

MacNeice's approach in *Solstices* is more varied. 'The Wiper' does indeed give the Grail-seeker modern transport without sacrificing the mystery of his journey into the unknown:

All we can see a segment
Of blackly shining asphalt
With the wiper moving across it
Clearing, blurring, clearing.

'Selva Oscura' reverts to a traditional mythic location for the Quest in its guise as self-pursuit: 'Lost in the maze / That means yourself'. The house in 'a clearing' represents return home in a more psychological (and tentative) sense than that of 'The Truisms': 'The door swings open and a hand / Beckons to all the life my days allow.' The journey poems, like the poems in general, veer between arrivals at 'clearings' and at greater darkness such as Charon 'black with obols' – although that too is a kind of clarification. They also veer between a Quest actively pursued (Roland's 'dedicated adventure') and the passive conveyance of Everyman to his doom. *Solstices*, despite 'Hold-up', contains more poems in which free will manages to remain in the driving seat. In *The Burning Perch* the conductor or cabby takes over. In 'Birthright', although the reluctant knight does not even mount his horse, the journey goes on despite him:

> The sun came up, my feet stuck fast,
> The minutes, hours, and years went past,
> More chances missed than I could count,
> The stable boys cried: 'Time to mount!'
> My jaw dropped and I gaped from drouth:
> My gift horse looked me in the mouth.

Like 'The Slow Starter', 'Birthright' implies that man may miss opportunities to control his destiny. Moreover, this parabolic fusion of 'nightmare' and 'gift horse' darkly inverts 'The world is what was given, / The world is what we make'. It also inverts the voyage poem 'Sailing Orders' (*Visitations*), which insists: 'And yet beliefs are still to make.' However, 'Thalassa', probably written after *The Burning Perch*, is another positive version of the *immram*, a rededication to the adventure of life:

> Put out to sea, ignoble comrades,
> Whose record shall be noble yet;
> Butting through scarps of moving marble
> The narwhal dares us to be free;
> By a high star our course is set,
> Our end is Life. Put out to sea.

That echoes the Gravedigger in *One for the Grave*. MacNeice's poetic Quest still had far to go when it was abruptly terminated. However, even the darknesses and dead-ends, hold-ups and hijackings, illuminate Everyman's predicament. MacNeice notes that 'either *Waiting for Godot* or *Endgame* could be described, if paradoxically, as a *static* quest' (*VP*, p. 119).

Solstices and *The Burning Perch* are just as socially conscious as

Autumn Journal. MacNeice criticized the parables of Edwin Muir for lacking socio-political grit as well as aesthetic grist: 'his metaphysico-mystical writing is so unadulterated either by topical or documentary elements or by primarily aesthetic ones, such as images used for their own sake, that I find reading many of his poems on end is like walking through a gallery of abstract paintings' (*VP*, pp. 124–5). Commenting on *Solstices*, he denies that he has become less 'committed' himself:

> My own position has been aptly expressed by the dying Mrs Gradgrind in Dickens's *Hard Times*: 'I think there's a pain somewhere in the room, but I couldn't positively say that I have got it.' So, whether these recent poems should be labelled 'personal' or 'impersonal', I feel that somewhere in the room there is a pain – and also, I trust, an alleviation. (*SCLM*, p. 224)

Similarly, noticing 'the high proportion of sombre pieces, ranging from bleak observations to thumbnail nightmares' in *The Burning Perch*, he remarks: 'Fear and resentment seem here to be serving me in the same way as Yeats in his old age claimed to be served by "lust and rage", and yet I had been equally fearful and resentful of the world we live in when I was writing *Solstices*' (*SCLM*, p. 247). MacNeice's travel poetry, which from *Visitations* onwards more successfully integrates impressions and judgements, is a measure of his disaffection. 'Old Masters Abroad' uses lecturing on English literature to sum up a dying colonialism: 'It is overtime now for the Old Masters'. In 'Ravenna' fallen Rome and Byzantine mosaics reactivate the mood of 'Spain / At Easter' rather than of Yeats's 'Sailing to Byzantium': 'What do I remember of Ravenna? / A bad smell mixed with glory, and the cold / Eyes that belie the tessellated gold'. Back home, an autumnal mood returns to London scenes. 'October in Bloomsbury' and 'Goodbye to London' suggest that here too the old masters are on overtime while the new masters have failed to build Utopia. 'Goodbye to London', which redeploys Dunbar's refrain about petals falling 'from the flower of cities all', traces a decline from wartime closeness to 'anticlimax' and diminishing hope that 'The phoenix would rise, for so they had promised'. In fact: 'nobody rose, only some meaningless / Buildings and the people once more were strangers'. Presumably this covers the entire postwar period, although MacNeice's gloom may have deepened with the defeat in 1951 of Clement Attlee's Labour government. He was also now at odds with the BBC.

Perhaps because both progress and Utopia have been finally exploded, the pain, fear and resentment in *The Burning Perch* savagely intensify MacNeice's thirties social critique. 'New Jerusalem' begins:

> Bulldoze all memories and sanctuaries: our birthright
> Means a new city, vertical, impersonal,
> Whose horoscope claimed a straight resurrection
> Should Stimulant stand in conjunction with Sleeping Pill.

This renews the lamentation of 'An Eclogue for Christmas' ('nothing comfortable remains / Un-improved, as flagging Rome improved villa and sewer'), but goes on to find no compensating 'beauty' in city lights or elsewhere. The critique also proceeds more obliquely, or as a dimension of larger parable. Poems like 'Flower Show', 'Pet Shop' and 'In Lieu' follow 'Birmingham' in projecting the victory of mechanistic and totalitarian forces. But instead of spraying the target, they take single symbols or ideas to nightmare extremes. Thus 'In Lieu', a poem which again broods on a cliché, pursues the logic of artificial replacement – no man tradition, god: 'In lieu therefore of choice / Thy Will be undone.' A final image of the obsolescence of ideals ('in lieu of a flag / The orator hangs himself from the flagpost') implies the poet's own role as unheeded prophet. So does the conclusion of 'Spring Cleaning', a poem in which even the newborn, are 'deaf incapsulated souls':

> While on a pillar in the sands
> A gaunt man scours his plinth and hauls
> His empty basket up and cries:
> Repent! It is time to round things off.

As the disaffected stylite in MacNeice retreats to the desert, he moves closer to the ancestral voice of Yeats as well as of Protestant evangelism. His protest about 'memories and sanctuaries' approaches Yeats's defence of 'Traditional sanctity and loveliness'. 'As in Their Time' includes this Yeatsian squib against the modern tide:

> Polyglot, albeit illiterate,
> He stood on a crumbling tower of Babel
> Cured of heredity, and though
> His idol had a brain of clay
> He could not read the cuneiform.

Similarly, 'Memoranda to Horace' (like the earlier 'To Posterity') warns that 'Dissolving dialects' threaten the durability of poetry itself.

The 'thumbnail nightmares' of 'As in Their Time', a microcosm of *The Burning Perch*, concentrate MacNeice's indictment of the contemporary world *sub specie aeternitatis*. At the centre of this mutant cosmos stands an artificial Everyman:

> Citizen of an ever-expanding
> Universe, burning smokeless fuel,
> He had lived among plastic gear so long
> When they decided to fingerprint him
> He left no fingerprints at all.

His female counterpart, 'a bundle of statistics', gets eaten by cannibals – which turns her 'skinfood' into a sick joke. Being 'Cured of heredity' involves loss of culture, loss of continuity (the old ladies left with 'nothing / To leave to the heirs that were dead before them'), loss of religion. These poems are certainly a case of absence implying need – not only of God. The last poem in the sequence, with its 'cloud no bigger than a god's hand', portends a nuclear Nemesis. In the meantime, neither personal relations ('She believed in love . . .') nor politics lead anywhere. Thirties idealism receives a wry epitaph in this self-enclosed, dwindling apologia:

> For what it was worth he had to
> Make a recurring protest:
> Which was at least a gesture

Which was a vindication
Or excuse for what it was worth.

The circular syntax epitomizes the economic, social, mental and moral tangles that trap these people. Outside the sequence 'The Suicide', a coded goodbye to the BBC and one of MacNeice's finest poems, contains an escape clause, if ambiguously framed:

And this, ladies and gentlemen, whom I am not in fact
Conducting, was his office all those minutes ago,
This man you never heard of. There are the bills
In the intray, the ash in the ashtray, the grey memoranda stacked
Against him, the serried ranks of the box-files, the packed
Jury of his unanswered correspondence
Nodding under the paperweight in the breeze
From the window by which he left; and here is the cracked
Receiver that never got mended and here is the jotter
With his last doodle which might be his own digestive tract
Ulcer and all or might be the flowery maze
Through which he had wandered deliciously till he stumbled
Suddenly finally conscious of all he lacked
On a manhole under the hollyhocks. The pencil
Point had obviously broken, yet, when he left this room
By catdrop sleight-of-foot or simple vanishing act,
To those who knew him for all that mess in the street
This man with the shy smile has left behind
Something that was intact.

Once again an Everyman exists amid voices: not only the unusually non-directive commentator on his life and works but the accusing 'grey memoranda', 'serried ranks' and 'packed / Jury'. The image of the 'last doodle', whether 'digestive tract' or 'flowery maze', points to the escape route of poetry itself. The doodle is another parable within a parable, open to alternative interpretations. 'Sleight-of-foot' connects with parable's own 'sleight of hand' and suggests that this 'vanishing act' may be one of creative rebellion. The language and imagery evoke 'The Individualist Speaks', the 'Judas kissing flowers' of 'Hidden Ice', and the escaping 'room and I' of 'Variation on Heraclitus'.

Among MacNeice's juvenilia is the remarkably Yeatsian 'Death of a Prominent Business Man' in which 'One of the wee folk out of the hills' calls the man away from 'stocks and shares' to a richer existence: 'And the old man's body lay dead in his chair, / But his soul had gone to taste the air / Away on the hills again'. 'Broken Windows' states: 'A poem in praise of suicide is an act of homage to life.' The 'fear and resentment' of *The Burning Perch* do not merely rehash the attitudes of poems MacNeice wrote in the 1930s. Rather, the culmination of thirties trends in the Cold War and the bomb has provoked a culmination of his earlier socio-political vision. In 'Budgie', as in other poems, thirties 'waiting for the end' has become an anticipation of final holocaust, a warning of Nemesis. This emblem of Everyman, 'attitudinizing' on his 'burning perch' before a solipsistic mirror, does not notice that 'The radio telescope / Picks up a quite different signal . . . the giant / Reptiles cackle in their graves.' The twenty-five years since MacNeice's death have made it clear how 'imbued with the true inner feel of [their] period' his parables are.

The Burning Perch also brings certain verbal techniques to a new pitch. Cliché and idiom tighten their control of poems – 'Déjà Vu', 'Round the Corner', 'In Lieu', 'Birthright'. The 'grave glade' of 'The Introduction' chills into a 'green grave'. At the end of 'Off the Peg', which shows some indulgence towards 'wellworn tunes', one cliché turns into another: 'And off the peg means made to measure now.' 'As in Their Time' exploits a variety of clichés as MacNeice perfects his touch with the modern riddle. Further, in keeping with the book's greater mythic density, he now draws more richly on the clichés of folk tradition – though not for their own sake. 'Children's Games' points out the anthropological giveaways in ritual chants: 'Catchum / Nigger by his whatnot round and round the launching site.' The conclusion of 'Sports Page' – 'And all our games funeral games' – holds not only for game-words but for MacNeice's word-games. 'Château Jackson' manages to include all human life within a nursery-rhyme formula and associated clichés. Notably, this poem too returns to its original metaphysical question, and so its 'quest' does not end but teasingly circles (like 'There's a hole in my bucket') without solution:

That bears the slab that wears the words
That tell the truth that ends the quest:
Where is the Jack that built the house?

As for the *sounds* of parable in *The Burning Perch*: syntax still plays a leading part in non-stanzaic poems, but finely diversified ('The Suicide') as well as strongly specialized ('Déjà Vu'). The most prominent metrical unit in the book, the quatrain, is sometimes a lurking presence. However, the verse technique that really comes into its own is the refrain, a technique with a folk-ghost. How much the refrain, or 'poetic repetition devices', had always appealed to MacNeice's ear is evident from his championship of Yeats's Crazy Jane poems:

> Irish folk songs and street ballads are very often refrained, and it was these models most probably which excited Yeats's emulation. But his use of the refrain is peculiar . . . A refrain . . . when it means anything, tends to be simpler in meaning than the rest of the poem; it gives the reader or hearer relief. Yeats's use of it, therefore, is often in two respects unusual. First the music of his refrain is often less obvious or smooth than that of the verses themselves, being sometimes flat, sometimes halting, sometimes strongly counterpointed. Secondly, his refrains tend to have either an intellectual meaning which is subtle and concentrated, or a symbolist or nonsense meaning which hits the reader below the belt. (*PWBY*, p. 147)

Yeats's practice struck home both to MacNeice's Irish roots and to his early love of all kinds of ballads. An example of a MacNeicean refrain with a 'subtle and concentrated intellectual meaning' is the chorus in 'The Habits' who reiterate that it's 'all for the best'. An example of 'symbolist or nonsense meaning' is 'crawly crawly' in 'The Introduction' (which sends shivers down the spine) or 'tra-la' in 'The Taxis'. The latter subverts what at first appears a traditionally straightforward refrain, just as the journey itself becomes weirder. Refrain often reinforces deterministic vistas in *The Burning Perch*, the sense that the universe runs on habitual tramlines. Thus 'Château Jackson' pushes its 'repetition-device' to a claustrophobic extreme. Conversely, the refrains of 'open' poems like 'Déjà Vu' and 'Round the Corner' heighten possibility as much as the iron 'in lieu' closes it down. It is difficult – and unnecessary – to decide where MacNeice's repetition-devices stop being true refrains and start being something else. The punctuation of 'Charon' by 'we just jogged on' and 'black with money . . . black with suspicion . . . black with obols' proves that refrain, like cliché (the two often coincide), does not merely 'colour' *The Burning Perch* but helps to construct it.

That the 'sombreness' of *The Burning Perch* took MacNeice by surprise gives the book no premonitory significance. Themes erupt unpredictably from the subterranean dynamic of lyric drama (Yeats was equally astonished by the 'bitterness' of *The Tower*). And if mortality now surfaces along with social pain, this primary obsession of MacNeice's had been making a comeback since *Visitations*. Like Yeats, MacNeice was born to write about ageing and death, but during the war he stopped being 'worried by the passage of time', and later his original imaginative tension between death and life slackened together with other antinomies. The mayflies no longer danced their defiance of petrifaction. But as his poetry took on the shape of 'a walking / Question', mortality was crucial to its renewed tensions. 'Age became real', as 'The Habits' puts it. So did nightmare: poems could no longer rely on sunlight coming to the rescue. Much of *The Burning Perch* is like discovering that waking up from the nightmare was only part of the dream. This recognition begins in *Visitations* which contains two fine poems about old people dying. 'House on a Cliff' unconsolingly depicts 'The strong man pained to find his red blood cools, / While the blind clock grows louder, faster'. 'Death of an Old Lady', an elegy for MacNeice's stepmother, perceives less dissonance between death and natural rhythms, into which it even manages to integrate the sinking of the Titanic: 'At eight in the evening the ship went down.' In 'Beni Hasan' age becomes personally real: 'It came to me on the Nile my passport lied / Calling me dark who am grey'. The poem goes on to concede ultimate victory to a version of 'granite sphinxes' encountered on their home ground. However, 'Dreams in Middle Age', would prefer to 'let nightmares whinny' if the alternative is static non-living, failure to be 'ourselves or more'. A better poem 'Windowscape' in *Solstices* embodies 'the dream of one lost soul' who 'feels neither alive nor dead'. These poems are conditioned more by the processes of ageing, fear of diminishing faculties, than by the fact of death. MacNeice's parables of stasis involve not only the absence of animating religious and social principles, but the absence of animation itself. 'Another Cold May' (about 'boredom') suggests bio-rhythms unable to assert themselves in the teeth of time: 'the square / Ahead remains ahead.' In 'Charon' too 'jogging on', slowing down while life goes on somewhere else, contrasts with the state of being a 'jigging' mayfly. However, in a sense all this realigns the contending forces of 'Mayfly'; changes emphases rather than fundamental insights. Being 'merely fifty' gave MacNeice new perspectives on relations between possibility and necessity. Retrospect deepened his understanding of Everyman's curriculum vitae, and 'Soap Suds' could not have come from the hand of a younger poet. But in opposition to 'Another Cold May' the love poems of *Solstices*, and 'To Mary' and 'Déjà Vu' in *The Burning Perch* celebrate the renewability of the life force: 'the gush / Of green . . . the wish to live' ('Solstice'). Thus the difference between the visions of a fully fleshed poem like 'Mayfly' and a 'skeletal' poem like 'The Introduction' is not straightforwardly historical, a progress from concord choreographed by mayflies to discords scored for crawly twigs above and cynical larvae below. The cosmos of *The Burning Perch* phrases the dark questions which a major poet must ask. As MacNeice says in 'Broken Windows': 'The "message" of a work of art may appear to be defeatist, negative, nihilist; the work of art itself is always *positive*.'

MacNeice concludes his remarks on the 'dialectic, oxymoron, irony' of *The Burning Perch*: 'I would venture the generalization that most of these poems are two-way affairs or at least spiral ones: even in the most evil picture the good things . . . are still there round the corner' (*SCLM*, p. 248). That makes it unnecessary to compute the balance of the opening windows and closed ambits, nightmares and surprises, which make up his overall Quest. However, 'Coda', with which he ended *The Burning Perch*, holds some kind of balance. 'Coda' is one of those poems that says everything: an Everyman parable uniting long-term and short-term human history, scepticism and belief:

> Maybe we knew each other better
> When the night was young and unrepeated
> And the moon stood still over Jericho.
>
> So much for the past; in the present
> There are moments caught between heart-beats
> When maybe we know each other better.

Whether life is regulated by God ('Jericho') or man ('heart-beats'), communion, communication, remains its desirable goal. The refrain's hypothetical form, and shifts of tense and position in fact keep MacNeice's 'mystical faith' alive. The symbolism of the last stanza derives from the meeting in 1962 of the two ends of the tunnel cut through Mont Blanc:

> But what is that clinking in the darkness?
> Maybe we shall know each other better
> When the tunnels meet beneath the mountain.

If an ultimate pattern is unknowable, 'Coda' condenses the spiral pattern of the Quest with its horizons of grave or grail. It also suggests how Louis MacNeice's poetry resonates in the darkness.

Select Bibliography

With abbreviations used in text

BY LOUIS MACNEICE

Collected Poems, ed. Eric Robertson Dodds, London, 1966
Selected Poems, ed. Michael Longley, London, 1988
Roundabout Way (under the pseudonym Louis Malone), London, 1932
Letters from Iceland (with W. H. Auden), London, 1937
I Crossed the Minch, London, 1938 (*ICTM*)
Modern Poetry: A Personal Essay, London, 1938, 1968 (*MP*)
Zoo, London, 1938
The Poetry of W. B. Yeats, London, 1941, 1967 (*PWBY*)
The Dark Tower and Other Radio Scripts London, 1947
The Mad Islands and *The Administrator*, London, 1964
The Strings are False: An Unfinished Autobiography, London, 1965 (*SAF*)
Varieties of Parable, Cambridge, 1965 (*VP*)
One for the Grave, London, 1968
Persons from Porlock and Other Plays for Radio, London, 1969
Selected Literary Criticism of Louis MacNeice, ed. Alan Heuser (with full bibliography of MacNeice's short prose), Oxford, 1987 (*SCLM*)
Selected Prose of Louis MacNeice, ed. Alan Heuser, Oxford, 1990
Selected Plays of Louis MacNeice, ed. Alan Heuser and Peter McDonald, Oxford, 1993

ABOUT LOUIS MACNEICE

Books
Brown, Terence, *Louis MacNeice: Sceptical Vision*, Dublin, 1975
Brown, Terence and Reid, Alec (eds.), *Time Was Away: The World of Louis MacNeice*, Dublin, 1974
Coulton, Barbara, *Louis MacNeice in the BBC*, London, 1980
McDonald, Peter, *Louis MacNeice: The Poet in his Contexts*, Oxford, 1991

McKinnon, William T., *Apollo's Blended Dream*, London, 1971
Marsack, Robyn, *The Cave of Making*, Oxford, 1982
Moore, D. B., *The Poetry of Louis MacNeice*, Leicester, 1972

Other books containing relevant material

Carter, Ronald (ed.), *Thirties Poets: 'The Auden Group'*, London, 1984
Cunningham, Valentine (ed.), *Spanish Front: Writers on the Civil War*, Oxford, 1986
Cunningham, Valentine, *British Writers of the Thirties*, Oxford, 1988
Davin, Dan, *Closing Times*, London, 1975
Dawe, Gerald, and Longley, Edna (eds.), *Across a Roaring Hill: The Protestant Imagination in Modern Ireland*, Belfast, 1985
Dodds E. R., *Missing Persons: An Autobiography*, Oxford, 1977
Dunn, Douglas (ed.), *Two Decades of Irish Writing*, Manchester, 1975
Grigson, Geoffrey, *Poems and Poets*, London, 1969
Grigson, Geoffrey (ed.), *Poetry of the Present*, London, 1949
Honest Ulsterman no. 73 (Louis MacNeice Number, September, 1983)
Hynes, Samuel, *The Auden Generation: Literature and Politics in England in the 1930s*, London, 1976 (*TAG*)
Longley, Edna, *Poetry in the Wars*, Newcastle upon Tyne, 1986
Longley, Edna, *The Living Stream: Literature and Revisionism in Ireland*, Newcastle upon Tyne, 1994
Lucas, John (ed.), *The Nineteen Thirties: A Challenge to Orthodoxy*, Brighton, 1978 (also available as Renaissance and Modern Studies XX, 1976)
Maxwell, D. E. S., *Poets of the Thirties*, London, 1969
Paulin, Tom, *Ireland and the English Crisis*, Newcastle upon Tyne, 1984
Scarfe, Francis, *Auden and After*, London, 1942
Spender, Stephen, *The Thirties and After*, London, 1978
Stallworthy, Jon, *Louis MacNeice*, London, 1995
Symons, Julian, *The Thirties: A Dream Revolved* (revised edn), London, 1975

Index